Ninja Air Fryer Max XL Cookbook 1000

Complete Guide of Ninja Air Fryer Cook Book for Beginners and Pros| Used to Fry, Roast, Broil, Bake, Reheat and Dehydrate| A 3-Week Meal Plan with 120 Recipes

By Dr. Johnson Wang

Table of Contents

Introduction

For many people, fried food is the absolute comfort food. Whether it's fried chicken, French fries, or fried street food, everyone has probably at least one fried food included on their guilt list.

Having tried it yourself, you know that frying makes your food taste delicious and crispy. However, while the flavor of foods burst in your mouth, sometimes you just can't help but think about how much calories you get from eating greasy foods.

Well, that's right, we all know how it's done. You need oil to fry, oftentimes, you need lots of it. And from what we know, too much oil on food is bad news. But did you know that it is actually possible to have tasty and crunchy food without having to drench your meal in oil?

Air fryers have become some of the hottest kitchen appliances today that make frying easier without the guilt. This kitchen gadget was invented to replace your traditional oil fryer with air to make it a healthy alternative to frying with oil. This new innovation has been gaining footing in many countries in the west and thus far has been making a difference in the way households prepare their food.

By definition, an air fryer is a kitchen appliance that cooks food by circulating hot air via convection mechanism. The hot air is circulated at high speed around the food by a mechanical fan, cooking the food and making it crispy.

In America, the grave effects of obesity have been associated with the consumption of too much oily food. The use of air fryers has been gaining praises due to its promising offer as a healthy solution to the long existing problem of obesity as a result of eating oil-filled food. Its auspicious contribution in the making a healthier lifestyle through healthy eating is what makes these types of gizmos very appealing especially to those who are trying to lose weight and those who are aiming for healthier living.

For those who can't live without fried food, using an air fryer is a good choice to cut down fat and calories from your food. Less oil means fewer calories.

Chapter 1: Essentials of Ninja Air Fryer Max XL

Do you ever find yourself short on time to cook? Perhaps, trying to cut down your weight but can't let go of those fatty food? Are you looking for a great kitchen tool to invest that can make any meal prep easier without much hassle?

When it comes to modern day cooking, one of the coolest gadgets that you can own in your household is an air fryer that does it all—a real ninja in the kitchen.

Ninja is one big name in the kitchen gadget scene. While it is best known for its blenders, this company is one of the best makers of the best air fryers in the market. With its sleek black design and high functionality of its air fryers, every unit looks great in any kitchen.

If you have been contemplating on whether an air fryer is worth the purchase, you may want to know what it does for you. At fingertips, you can have an appliance that can imitate foods made in oil fryers, only that it is healthier and guilt-free with Ninja Air Fryer Max XL. This air fryer will serves up many ways in making life easier. Definitely a wise choice for every household.

What is Ninja Air Fryer Max XL?

Ninja Air Fryer Max XL (Ninja AF161 Series) offers a fast and easy way of preparing your favorite food.

This Ninja fryer can cook your favorite food to crisp using little to no oil, making food preparation healthier.

Skip the take-out and prepare tasty and healthy fried meals minus the guilt in a flash. This appliance fries up with 75% less fat than any other frying methods. Less oils, less calories.

How the Ninja Air Fryer Max XL Works?

Ninja Air Fryer Max XL uses Max Crisp Technology that cooks food for up to 30 percent faster than the Ninja AF100 Series.

It has a family-sized 5.5-qt basket can cook up to 3-lb French fries, chicken tenders and more and make them crunchy and chewy in no time minus the grease.

Aside from air frying, its other functions include **Max Crisp, Air Roast, Air Broil, Bake, Reheat and Dehydrate.**

Make healthy meals in a flash with this Ninja Air Fryer series.

Is Ninja Air Fryer Max XL Better Than Normal Air Fryer?

Most air fryers replace traditional deep fryers due to its promising benefits as far as food quality and convenience are concerned. However, not all air fryers offer the same quality, so it is important to choose the right product for you to get the best out of this great kitchen innovation.

Since the invention of this genius gadget, there are now a lot of air fryers that exist in the market claiming to be the best appliance that suit your cooking needs so it all boils down to quality.

Ninja Air Fryer Max XL works like a real ninja. It cooks your food perfectly and fast plus it's easy to use by anyone in the household. This unit offers a simple set of push-button controls of its functions that works immediately at one press of your fingertips. It has various cooking functions that easily activates with a push of the button. Select from max crisp, air fry, air roast, air broil, bake, reheat, and dehydrate.

The Ninja Air Fryers Series has multi-function features. The number of functions varies between air fryer models. The Ninja Air Fryer Max XL is bigger in dimension so it fits a lot of food that you can cook at once.

Ninja Air Fryer Max XL delivers 110 degrees to 450 degrees of superheated air that turns food into a scrumptious meal.

It works by circulating hot air around the food using the convection mechanism. A built-in mechanical fan circulates the hot air around the food at high speed, cooking the food and producing a crispy layer via browning reactions.

This ninja air fryer allows food to be cooked on its own oil and releasing them which lessens the oil content for a guilt-free fried meal favorites.

Buttons and Functions

The Ninja Air Fryer Max XL offers button controls that are easy to use so that anyone can operate it.

Cooking Functions Buttons

Max Crisp

Select this function to give frozen foods extra crispiness and crunch with little to no oil.

Air Fry

Use this function to give food crispiness and crunch with little to no oil.

Air Roast

This can be used to roast tender meats, vegetables, and more.

Air Broil

Use this function to caramelize and brown food.

Bake

Select this function to create decedent baked treats and desserts such as tarts and cookies.

Reheat

Functions similar to a microwave that heats leftovers by gently warming them, leaving you with crispy, fresh tasting heated food.

Dehydrate

Use this function to dehydrate meats, fruits, and vegetables for healthy snacks.

Operating Buttons

The Ninja Air Fryer Max XL has operating buttons that are easy to use in setting up functions and cooking settings.

Temp Arrows

Adjust the cooking temperature for any function by pressing the UP and DOWN buttons before or during cooking. Preheat the fryer by setting the temperature using these buttons.

Time Arrows

Adjust the cooking time for any function using the UP and DOWN buttons.

Start/Stop Button

After setting the time and temperature, press START/STOP button to start cooking. Press the same button to stop cooking.

Power Button

Turn ON/OFF the unit by pressing the Power button. This also stops all cooking modes of the fryer.
Ninja Air Fryer Max XL is strategically designed to provide convenience in cooking. Its unit design and features are easy to operate for a no mess no stress food preparation.

Before Using Ninja Air Fryer Max XL

How to Use it Properly

➤ Remove and discard all the unnecessary packaging material from the unit. Remove all accessories from the package.
➤ Read the user's manual carefully. Pay close attention to operational instructions, warnings, and important safeguards to safely use the unit and avoid accidents.
➤ Wash the ceramic-coated basket, crisper plate, and accessories in hot, soapy water, then rinse and dry thoroughly before using. NEVER clean the main unit in the dishwasher.

Using the Cooking Functions

Plug the power cord into a wall outlet and press the Power button to turn on the unit.

Max Crisp

1. Attach the crisper plate in the basket.
2. Press the MAX CRISP button. The default temperature setting will be displayed on the screen. (The temperature setup CANNOT be changed in this function.)
3. Set the cooking time by pressing the TIME buttons.
4. Add the ingredients to be cooked to the basket. Insert the basket in the unit.
5. Press START/STOP button to start cooking.
6. Remove the basket and toss the ingredients. (The unit will pause cooking automatically when the basket is removed and will resume once the basket is reinserted.)
7. The unit will beep and END will display on the control panel when cooking is complete.
8. Remove the ingredients from the basket.

Note: For best results, preheat the fryer for 3 minutes before adding the ingredients.

Air Fry

1. Attach the crisper plate in the basket.
2. Press the AIR FRY button. The default temperature setting will be displayed on the screen. Set the desired frying temperature using the TEMP buttons.
3. Set the frying time by pressing the TIME buttons.
4. Add the ingredients to be cooked to the basket. Insert the basket in the unit.
5. Press START/STOP button to start cooking.
6. Remove the basket and toss the ingredients. (The unit will pause cooking automatically when the basket is removed and will resume once the basket is reinserted.)
7. The unit will beep and END will display on the control panel when frying is complete.
8. Remove the ingredients from the basket.

Note: For best results, preheat the fryer for 3 minutes before adding the ingredients.

Air Roast

1. Attach the crisper plate in the basket.
2. Press the AIR ROAST button. The default temperature setting will be displayed on the screen. Set the desired roasting temperature using the TEMP buttons.
3. Set the roasting time by pressing the TIME buttons.
4. Add the ingredients to be cooked to the basket. Insert the basket in the unit.
5. Press START/STOP button to start cooking.
6. Remove the basket and toss the ingredients. (The unit will pause cooking automatically when the basket is removed and will resume once the basket is reinserted.)
7. The unit will beep and END will display on the control panel when roasting is complete.
8. Remove the ingredients from the basket.

Note: For best results, preheat the fryer for 3 minutes before adding the ingredients.

Air Broil

1. Attach the crisper plate in the basket.
2. Press the AIR BROIL button. The default temperature setting will be displayed on the screen. Set the desired broiling temperature using the TEMP buttons.
3. Set the broiling time by pressing the TIME buttons.
4. Add the ingredients to be cooked to the basket. Insert the basket in the unit. Recommended: Preheat heater for 3 minutes before adding ingredients
5. Press START/STOP button to start cooking.
6. Remove the basket and toss the ingredients. (The unit will pause cooking automatically when the basket is removed and will resume once the basket is reinserted.)
7. The unit will beep and END will display on the control panel when broiling is complete.
8. Remove the ingredients from the basket.

Note: For best results, use the broil rack. When using the broil rack, do not layer food below the rack.

Bake

1. Attach the crisper plate in the basket.
2. Press the BAKE button. The default temperature setting will be displayed on the screen. Set the desired baking temperature using the TEMP buttons.
3. Set the baking time by pressing the TIME buttons.
4. Add the ingredients to be cooked to the basket. Insert the basket in the unit. Recommended: Preheat heater for 3 minutes before adding ingredients
5. Press START/STOP button to start cooking.
6. The unit will beep and END will display on the control panel when baking is complete.
7. Remove the ingredients from the basket.

Note: To convert recipes from a conventional oven, reduce the temperature of the air fryer by 25°F. Check food frequently to avoid overcooking.

Reheat

1. Attach the crisper plate in the basket.
2. Press the REHEAT button. The default temperature setting will be displayed on the screen. Set the desired reheating temperature using the TEMP buttons.
3. Set there heating time by pressing the TIME buttons.
4. Add the ingredients to be cooked to the basket. Insert the basket in the unit.   Press START/STOP button to start cooking.
5. The unit will beep and END will display on the control panel when reheating is complete.
6. Remove the ingredients from the basket.

Dehydrate

1. Arrange the layer of ingredients in the bottom of the basket then install the crisper plate for a set of second layer of ingredients.
2. Press the DEHYDRATE button. The default temperature setting will be displayed on the screen. Set the desired dehydrating temperature using the TEMP buttons.
3. Set the dehydrating time by pressing the TIME buttons.
4. Add the ingredients to be cooked to the basket. Insert the basket in the unit.   Press START/STOP button to start cooking.
5. The unit will beep and END will display on the control panel when dehydrating is complete.
6. Remove the ingredients from the basket.

Note: You can increase your air fryer's dehydrating capacity with the mid-level rack.

Where to Shop For it

The Ninja Air Fryer Max XL can be purchased at Amazon at a retail price of $139.99. This Ninja Air Fryer is rated 4.7 out of 5 stars in Amazon.

Safety Guide on Using it

Here is a guide on how to safely use the Ninja Air Fryer Max XL:

➢ Read the user's manual to know how to operate the unit.
➢ Always ensure that all the parts of the appliance are properly assembled before use.
➢ Make sure that the air intake vent or air socket vent are not blocked while the unit is running. Doing so may cause overheat to the unit or may facilitate uneven cooking.
➢ Ensure that the removable ceramic coated basket is clean and dry before placing it into the main unit.
➢ The Ninja Air Fryer Max XL is made for household use only. Do not use outdoors.
➢ This unit is intended for worktop use only. Ensure that the surface is clean, dry and leveled. Do not move the unit when in use.
➢ Do not touch hot surface. Always wear protective hot pads or oven mitts when using the appliance to prevent burns or personal injury.
➢ Do not place the appliance near hot surfaces and flammables such as hot gas or electric burner.
➢ If the unit emits black smoke, unplug the unit immediately and wait for the smoking to stop before taking out the other accessories.

How to Clean Your Air Fryer Max XL

Always ensure that the accessories are clean and dry before and after every use.

➢ Unplug the unit prior to cleaning. Never immerse the main unit in water or any other liquid or place in a dishwasher.
➢ Clean the main unit and the control panel with a damp cloth. While the basket, crisper plate and other accessories can be washed with water or can be cleaned in the dishwasher.
➢ If food is stuck on the crisper plate or basket, allow it to smoke in warm soapy water to soften the residues.
➢ Air- dry or towel-dry all parts after cleaning.

Amazing Tips and Tricks on Using it

1. Do not overcrowd the ingredients.

To facilitate even cooking and browning, make sure the ingredients are properly arranged and do not overlap in the basket. Check the food and shake the basket for even browning.

2. Convert oven recipes.

Convert oven recipes by reducing the temperature of the fryer by 25°F. check the   check progress frequently to avoid overcooking. Remove food when desired level of brownness has been achieved.

3. Preheat

Preheat the fryer for 3 minutes before placing the ingredients to ensure even temperature inside the unit.

4. Secure your food.

Secure lightweight foods with toothpicks inside the fryer as they may be blown inside by the mechanical fan.

5. Add more crisp.

Use the crisper plate to improve crispiness of the ingredients. The crisper plate will lift the ingredients in the basket so air can circulate all over the food for a more crisp result.

6. Add a bit of oil.

When cooking fresh vegetables, use at least 1 tablespoon of oil and add more to achieve a preferred level of crispine

Dehydrate Tips & Tricks

1. Make thin slices.

Make thin slices to achieve perfectly dehydrated food slices. To make consistent thin slices, use a mandoline slice to get thin fruits and vegetable slices.

2. Dry your ingredients.

Pat the ingredients dry before placing them in the basket to remove excess moisture or liquids.

3. Trim off the fat.

Fat does not dry out and may turn rancid. Trim off the fat of the beef or poultry before dehydrating them.

4. Do not overcrowd.

Lay the ingredients flat on the basket, closely as possible but not overlapping. Optimize the space to avoid uneven drying of the ingredients.

5. Use Roast Function to pasteurize jerky.

When dehydrating meats, finish it off by using the Roast function at 330°F for 1 minute to fully pasteurize the dried meat.

6. Store the dried ingredients well.

FAQS

Store the dehydrated foods at room temperature in an airtight container for up to 2 weeks to maximize its shelf lie.

1. How high can the temperature of the fryer go?

For Max Crisp and Air boil, the temperature can go at a maximum of 450 degrees F while the max temperature for all function is 400 degrees F.

2. How long do I need to preheat the air fryer? How will I know when it's done?

To preheat, select the function, time and temperature of the air fryer, and press START/STOP. We recommend preheating the fryer for 3 minutes.

3. What are the cooking functions included in the unit?

The air fryer unit has 7 different cooking functions: Max Crisp, Air Broil, Air Fry, Dehydrate, Air Roast, Bake, and Reheat (Max Crisp and Air Broil not included in all models).

4. Should you defrost the frozen foods before air frying?

This depends on the kind of food you are going to fry. For frozen meats, it's better to defrost them first prior to air drying.

5. When should I add the ingredients? Can I put the item before or after preheating?

Allow the unit to preheat first for at least 3 minutes prior to adding the ingredients to get best result.

6. How do I pause the countdown?

Removing the basket from the unit will automatically pause the timer. If you want to totally stop the cooking function, press START/STOP to reset the timer.

7. Is the basket non-stick? When do I use the crisper plate?

The basket is made from aluminum with a non-stick ceramic coating. The crisper plate raises the food in the basket to allow air to flow under it as it cooks, this way your food is cooked evenly and turns out crispy.

8. My food didn't cook well. Why?

The cook time and temperature can be adjusted at any time. Check your food a few times while it cooks. Simply press the TIME or TEMP buttons and rotate the dial. Make sure to arrange the ingredients in the basket in an even layer. Do not overlap the ingredients so it will brown evenly on all sides. Always make sure that the basket is fully inserted as it cooks.

9. Why did my food burn?

To avoid overcooking, check progress throughout cooking to see how your food is. Remove the food from the basket once you get your desired outcome.

10. Can I air fry fresh battered foods?

Yes, but the ingredients need to be breaded properly. It needs to be coated flour, egg and crumbs in a way that it sticks properly in place unto the food pieces. Loose breading may be blown off by the fryer's fan. The food must not be wetly coated with the batter as well as it will only run down and will stick to the basket instead as it fries.

11. Why do some ingredients get blown when air frying?

The fryer has a fan inside which may blow lightweight foods around. You can use

12. The screen suddenly went black. What happened?

If the screen turns black when you didn't turn it off means it went on standby mode. Press the power button to turn it back on.

13. What does the beeping of the unit means?

When the timer sets off, the unit will start beeping indicating the cooking function is complete.

14. What does an "E" on the display screen means?

This indicates ERROR and the unit may not be functioning properly.

Air Fry Cooking Chart for the AF100 Series Ninja Air Fryer

Ingredient	Amount	Preparation	Toss in Oil	Temperature	Cook Time
Asparagus	2 bunches	Whole, trim stems	2 tsp	390°F	11–13 mins
Beets	6 small or 4 large (about 2 lbs)	Whole	None	390°F	45–60 mins
Bell peppers (for roasting)	4 peppers	Whole	None	400°F	26–30 mins
Broccoli	1 head	Cut in 1-inch florets	1 Tbsp	390°F	13–16 mins
Carrots	2 lbs	Peel, cut in 1/2-inch pieces	1 Tbsp	400°F	20–24 mins
Cauliflower	2 heads	(about 2 lbs) Cut in 1-inch florets	2 Tbsp	390°F	20–24 mins
Corn on the cob	4 ears	Whole, remove husks	1 Tbsp	390°F	12–15 mins
Chicken wings	3 lbs	Drumettes & flats	1 Tbsp	390°F	22–26 mins
Salmon fillets	2 fillets (4 oz each)	None	Brush with oil	390°F	10–13 mins
Steaks	2 steaks (8 oz each)	Whole	None	390°F	10–20 mins

Dehydrate Chart for the AF100 Series Ninja Air Fryers

Ingredient	Preparation	Temperature	Cook Time
Apples	Core removed, cut in 1/8 slices, Rinsed In lemon water, patted dry	135°F	7-8 hrs
Asparagus	Cut in 1-inch pieces, blanched	135°F	6-8 hrs
Bananas	Peeled Cut in 3/8 inch-slices	135°F	8-10 hrs
Beets	Peeled Cut in 1/8 inch-slices	135°F	6-8 hrs
Eggplant	Peeled, cut in 1/4 inch slice, blanched	135°F	6-8 hrs
Tomatoes	Cut in 3/8 inch slice, grated, steam if planning to rehydrate	135°F	
Beef Jerky	Cut 1/4 inch slice, marinated overnight	150°F	5-7 hrs
Chicken Jerky	Cut 1/4 inch slice, marinated overnight	150°F	5-7 hrs
Turkey Jerky	Cut 1/4 inch slice, marinated overnight	150°F	5-7 hrs
Salmon	Cut 1/4 inch slice, marinated overnight	150°F	3-5 hrs

Air Fry Cooking Chart for the AF160 Series Ninja Air Fryer

Ingredient	Amount	Preparation	Toss in Oil	Temperature	Cook Time
Asparagus	1 bunch	Whole, stems trimmed	2 tsp	390°F	8–12 mins
Beets	6 small or 4 large (about 2 lbs)	Whole	None	390°F	45–60 mins
Mushrooms	8 oz Rinsed,	cut in quarters	1 Tbsp	390°F	7–9 mins
Zucchini	1 lb	Cut in quarters lengthwise, then cut in 1-inch pieces	1 Tbsp	390°F	15–18 mins
Chicken breasts	2 breasts (3/4–1 1/2 lbs each)	Bone in	Brushed with oil	375°F	25–35 mins
Burgers	4 quarter-pound patties	80% lean 1 inch thick	None	375°F	8–10 mins
French fries	2 lb	None	None	360°F	28–32 mins
Fish fillets	1 box (6 fillets)	None	None	390°F	14–16 mins
Pizza rolls	1 bag (20 oz, 40 count)	None	None	390°F	12–15 mins
Green beans	1 bag (12 oz)	Trimmed	1 Tbsp	390°F	8–10 mins
Bacon	4 strips, cut in half	None	None	350°F	8–10 mins

Max Crisp Cooking Chart for the AF160 Series Ninja Air Fryers

Ingredient	Amount	Preparation	Toss in Oil	Cook Time
Chicken nuggets	1 box (12 oz)	None	None	7–9 mins
Chicken wings	2 lbs (32 oz)	None	1 Tbsp	25 mins
French fries	1 lb (16 oz)	None	None	15 mins
French fries	2 lbs (32 oz)	None	None	25 mins
Mini corn dogs	14 oz (20–24 ct)	None	None	6 mins
Mini corn dogs	24 oz (40–46 ct)	None	None	8–10 mins
Mozzarella sticks	24 oz	None	None	6–8 mins
Pizza rolls	1 bag (20 oz, 40 ct)	None	None	6–8 mins
Pot stickers	24 oz (20–24 ct)	None	None	8–10 mins
Mozzarella sticks	24 oz	None	None	6–8 mins

Chapter 2: A 3-Week Ninja Air Fry Meal Plan

Here's a list of some of the most common things that you'll need for air frying:

- ✓ Cooking spray
- ✓ Vegetable oil
- ✓ Salt and pepper
- ✓ Herbs and spices
- ✓ Panko breadcrumbs

- ✓ Flour
- ✓ Eggs
- ✓ Vegetables
- ✓ Meat, poultry, fish and seafood

Week 1

Sunday

- ➤ Breakfast: Sweet Potato Hash
- ➤ Lunch: Pizza Hot Dogs
- ➤ Dinner: Coconut Shrimp

Monday

- ➤ Breakfast: Mexican Hash Browns
- ➤ Lunch: Buttermilk Fried Chicken
- ➤ Dinner: Pepper Shrimp

Tuesday

- ➤ Breakfast: Breakfast Sausage
- ➤ Lunch: Rib Eye Steak
- ➤ Dinner: Crispy Cod

Wednesday

- ➤ Breakfast: Bacon

- ➤ Lunch: Eggplant Parmesan
- ➤ Dinner: Herbed Turkey

Thursday

- ➤ Breakfast: Garlic Cheese Bread
- ➤ Lunch: Tuna Patties
- ➤ Dinner: Roasted Asparagus & Mushrooms

Friday

- ➤ Breakfast: Ham & Egg Tarts
- ➤ Lunch: Roasted Cauliflower & Broccoli
- ➤ Dinner: Baby Back Ribs

Saturday

- ➤ Breakfast: French Toast Sticks
- ➤ Lunch: Tender & Juicy Pork Chops
- ➤ Dinner: Honey Spicy Chicken Wings

Week 2

Sunday

- ➤ Breakfast: Churros
- ➤ Lunch: Meatballs in Tomato Sauce
- ➤ Dinner: Ranch Chicken Nuggets

Monday

- ➤ Breakfast: Breakfast Sausage
- ➤ Lunch: Lemon Rosemary Fish
- ➤ Dinner: Spicy Green Beans

Tuesday

- Breakfast: Ham & Egg Tarts
- Lunch: Breaded Shrimp
- Dinner: Salmon Cakes with Spicy Mayo

Wednesday

- Breakfast: French Toast Sticks
- Lunch: Steak & Mushrooms
- Dinner: Roasted Brussels Sprouts

Thursday

- Breakfast: Breakfast Frittata
- Lunch: Buttered Fish
- Dinner: Lamb Meatballs

Friday

- Breakfast: Mexican Hash Browns
- Lunch: Blackened Chicken
- Dinner: Fish with Pesto

Saturday

- Breakfast: Scotch Eggs
- Lunch: Roasted Veggies
- Dinner: Eggplant Parmesan

Week 3

Sunday

- Breakfast: French Toast Sticks
- Lunch: Salmon Patties
- Dinner: Roasted Asparagus & Mushrooms

Monday

- Breakfast: Breakfast Frittata
- Lunch: Ranch Pork Chops
- Dinner: Zucchini Gratin

Tuesday

- Breakfast: Ham & Egg Tarts
- Lunch: Potato Latkes
- Dinner: Peruvian Chicken

Wednesday

- Breakfast: Breakfast Sausage
- Lunch: Sweet Salmon
- Dinner: Roasted Veggies

Thursday

- Breakfast: Mexican Hash Browns
- Lunch: Steak Strips with Mushrooms
- Dinner: Roasted Cauliflower

Friday

- Breakfast: Churros
- Lunch: Garlic Chicken
- Dinner: Lemon Rosemary Fish

Saturday

- Breakfast: Breakfast Frittata
- Lunch: Salmon Patties
- Dinner: Cajun Pork Chops

Measurement Conversions

Measure	Equivalent
1/16 teaspoon	Dash
1/8 teaspoon	Pinch
3 teaspoons	1 tablespoon
1/8 cup	2 tablespoons

1/4 cup	4 tablespoons
1/3 cup	5 tablespoons plus 1 teaspoon
1/2 cup	8 tablespoons
3/4 cup	12 tablespoons
1 cup	16 tablespoons
1 pound	16 ounces
8 fluid ounces	1 cup
1 pint	2 cups
1 quart	2 pints or 4 cups
1 teaspoon	5 ml
1 tablespoon	15 ml
1 fluid oz.	30 ml
1/5 cup	50 ml
1 cup	240 ml
1 oz.	28 grams
1 pound	454 grams

Chapter 3: 15 Breakfast and Lunch Recipes

Sweet Potato Hash

Serves: 6
Preparation and Cooking Time: 25 minutes

Ingredients:

2 slices bacon, chopped
2 sweet potatoes, cubed
1 tablespoon smoked paprika
2 tablespoons olive oil
1 teaspoon dried dill weed
Salt and pepper to taste

Preparation:

1. Preheat your Ninja air fryer to 400 degrees F.
2. Toss all the ingredients in a bowl.
3. Transfer to the air fryer.
4. Cook for 15 minutes, stirring every 3 minutes.

Serving Suggestion:

Garnish with chopped parsley or chives.

Tip:

You can also use chopped ham instead of bacon.

Nutritional Information Per Serving:

Calories: 191
Total Fat: 6g
Saturated Fat: 1.0g
Cholesterol: 3mg
Sodium: 447mg
Potassium: 566mg
Total Carbohydrates: 31.4g
Dietary Fiber: 5.1g
Protein: 3.7g
Sugars: 6g

Breakfast Frittata

Serves: 2
Preparation and Cooking Time: 35 minutes

Ingredients:

4 eggs, beaten
1 green onion, chopped
2 tablespoons bell pepper, chopped
1/2 cup cheddar cheese
1/4 lb. breakfast sausage, cooked, removed from casing and crumbled
Cooking spray

Preparation:

1. Mix all the ingredients in a bowl.
2. Preheat your air fryer to 360 degrees F and spray with oil.
3. Pour the egg mixture into a small cake pan.
4. Place inside the air fryer.
5. Cook for 20 minutes.

Serving Suggestion:

Sprinkle fresh herbs on top.

Nutritional Information Per Serving:

Calories: 380
Total Fat: 27.4g
Saturated Fat: 12.0g
Cholesterol: 443mg
Sodium: 694mg
Potassium: 328mg
Total Carbohydrates: 2.9g
Dietary Fiber: 0.4g
Protein: 31.2g
Sugars: 1g

Mexican Hash Browns

Serves: 4
Preparation and Cooking Time: 1 hour and 5 minutes

Ingredients:

2 lb. potatoes, cubed and soaked in water for 20 minutes
1 tablespoon olive oil, divided
1 red bell pepper, chopped
1 jalapeno pepper, sliced into rings
1 onion, chopped
1/2 teaspoon ground cumin
1/2 teaspoon taco seasoning mix
Salt and pepper to taste

Preparation:

1. Preheat your air fryer to 320 degrees F.
2. Toss the potatoes in half of the oil.
3. Cook in the air fryer for 20 minutes, shaking every 5 minutes.
4. In a bowl, add the rest of the ingredients.
5. Mix well.
6. Add to the air fryer and cook for another 5 minutes.

Serving Suggestion:

Garnish with lemon wedges.

Tip

Use fresh potatoes to create crispy hash browns.

Nutritional Information Per Serving:

Calories: 267
Total Fat: 13g
Saturated Fat: 8g
Cholesterol: 227mg
Sodium: 571mg
Potassium: 750mg
Total Carbohydrates: 7g
Dietary Fiber: 3g
Protein: 17g
Sugars: 1g

French Toast Sticks

Serves: 2
Preparation and Cooking Time: 20 minutes
Ingredients:

1/4 cup almond milk
2 eggs, beaten
1 teaspoon cinnamon

1 teaspoon vanilla extract

4 slices bread, sliced into sticks

Preparation:

1. Preheat your Ninja air fryer to 360 degrees F.
2. Mix all the ingredients in a bowl except the bread.
3. Dip the bread sticks into the mixture.
4. Cook in the air fryer basket in batches, for 10 minutes each batch, turning halfway through.

Serving Suggestion:

Dust with confectioners' sugar.

Tip:

Dry bread completely before using.

Nutritional Information Per Serving:

Calories: 231
Total Fat: 7.4g
Saturated Fat: 2.0g
Cholesterol: 188mg
Sodium: 423mg
Potassium: 173mg
Total Carbohydrates: 28.6g
Dietary Fiber: 1.9g
Protein: 11.2g
Sugars: 4g

Breakfast Sausage

Serves: 4

Preparation and Cooking Time: 15 minutes

Ingredients:

12 oz. sausage patties

Cooking spray

Preparation:

1. Preheat your air fryer to 400 degrees F.
2. Add the patties in the air fryer basket and spray with oil.
3. Cook for 5 minutes.
4. Turn and cook for another 4 minutes.

Serving Suggestion:

Serve with whole wheat burger buns.

Tip:

Add chopped lettuce or sliced tomatoes to make a sandwich.

Nutritional Information Per Serving:

Calories: 145
Total Fat: 9g
Saturated Fat: 3.0g
Cholesterol: 46mg
Sodium: 393mg
Potassium: 228mg
Total Carbohydrates: 0.7g
Dietary Fiber: 0g
Protein: 14.1g
Sugars: 1g

Ham & Egg Tarts

Serves: 4

Preparation and Cooking Time: 30 minutes

Ingredients:

1 sheet puffy pastry

4 tablespoons cheese, shredded

4 tablespoons ham, cooked and diced

4 eggs

Preparation:

1. Preheat your air fryer to 400 degrees F.
2. Slice puffy pastry into 4.

3. Place in the air fryer basket for 6 minutes.
4. Make an indentation in the puffy pastry.
5. Add cheese and ham on top.
6. Add the egg on top.
7. Cook for 5 minutes.

Serving Suggestion:

Garnish with chopped fresh chives

Nutritional Information Per Serving:

Calories: 446
Total Fat: 31g
Saturated Fat: 9.0g
Cholesterol: 199mg
Sodium: 377mg
Potassium: 137mg
Total Carbohydrates: 27.9g
Dietary Fiber: 0.9g
Protein: 14.2g
Sugars: 1g

Churros

Serves: 6
Preparation and Cooking Time: 25 minutes

Ingredients:

1/2 cup milk
1/4 cup butter, melted
Salt to taste
1/2 cup all-purpose flour
2 eggs
1/4 cup sugar
1/2 teaspoon ground cinnamon

Preparation:

1. Mix milk, butter and salt in a pan over medium heat.
2. Add the flour and egg, and mix well.
3. Transfer mixture into a pastry bag.
4. Pipe the dough to create strips and cook in the air fryer for 5 minutes.
5. Combine cinnamon and sugar in a bowl.
6. Sprinkle the churros with this mixture.

Serving Suggestion:

Dust with confectioners' sugar.

Tip:

Pipe dough directly into the air fryer basket

Nutritional Information Per Serving:

Calories: 172
Total Fat: 9.8g
Saturated Fat: 6.0g
Cholesterol: 84mg
Sodium: 112mg
Potassium: 67mg
Total Carbohydrates: 17.5g
Dietary Fiber: 0.4g
Protein: 3.9g
Sugars: 9g

Bacon

Serves: 6
Preparation and Cooking Time: 15 minutes

Ingredients:

16 oz. bacon

Preparation:

1. Preheat your air fryer to 390 degrees F.

2. Add the bacon to the air fryer basket.
3. Cook for 7 minutes.
4. Flip and cook for 8 minutes.

Serving Suggestion:

Serve with omelette, frittata or fresh green salad.

Tip:

Extend cooking to make bacon crispier.

Nutritional Information Per Serving:

Calories: 173
Total Fat: 17g
Saturated Fat: 6.0g
Cholesterol: 26mg
Sodium: 315mg
Potassium: 79mg
Total Carbohydrates: 0.2g
Dietary Fiber: 0g
Protein: 4.4g
Sugars: 0g

Scotch Eggs

Serves: 6
Preparation and Cooking Time: 30 minutes

Ingredients:

Sauce:
3 tablespoons mango flavored yogurt
1 tablespoon mayonnaise
Salt and pepper to taste
Pinch curry powder
Eggs:
1 lb. pork sausage
6 hard-boiled eggs, peeled
1/4 cup flour
2 eggs, beaten
1 cup panko bread crumbs
Cooking spray

Preparation:

1. Mix the sauce ingredients and refrigerate.
2. Create 6 patties from the ground pork.
3. Wrap the hardboiled eggs with the patties.
4. Dip in the beaten eggs and cover with breadcrumbs.
5. Place these in the air fryer.
6. Cook at 390 degrees F for 12 minutes or until crispy.
7. Serve with the sauce.

Serving Suggestion:

Let cool and slice in half before serving.

Tip:

Add all sauce ingredients in food processor and blend until smooth.

Nutritional Information Per Serving:

Calories: 407
Total Fat: 27.8g
Saturated Fat: 9.0g
Cholesterol: 284mg
Sodium: 945mg
Potassium: 308mg
Total Carbohydrates: 21.5g
Dietary Fiber: 0.4g
Protein: 21.4g
Sugars: 3g

Potato Latkes

Serves: 5
Preparation and Cooking Time: 40 minutes

Ingredients:

16 oz. hash browns
1/2 cup onion, grated
1 egg, beaten
Salt and pepper to taste
2 tablespoons breadcrumbs
Cooking spray

Preparation:

1. Preheat your air fryer to 375 degrees F.
2. Squeeze moisture out of the onion and hash browns.
3. Season the egg with the salt and pepper.
4. Add the potatoes and the breadcrumbs.
5. Mix well.
6. Form patties from the mixture.
7. Spray air fryer basket with oil.
8. Transfer patties in the air fryer basket.
9. Cook for 10 minutes or until golden.

Serving Suggestion:

Serve with apple sauce or sour cream.

Tip:

Use avocado oil spray to give the latkes a golden finish.

Nutritional Information Per Serving:

Calories: 97
Total Fat: 6.5g
Saturated Fat: 2.0g
Cholesterol: 33mg
Sodium: 121mg
Potassium: 439mg
Total Carbohydrates: 18.6g
Dietary Fiber: 1.6g
Protein: 3.3g
Sugars: 1g

Salmon Patties

Serves: 4
Preparation and Cooking Time: 25 minutes

Ingredients:

Sauce:
1/2 teaspoon lemon juice
1/2 cup light mayonnaise
2 pinches Cajun seasoning
1 teaspoon garlic, minced
Patties:
12 oz. salmon, flaked or chopped
1 tablespoon chives, chopped
1 teaspoon parsley, chopped
1 teaspoon garlic, minced
Salt to taste
1 tablespoon flour
Cooking spray

Preparation:

1. Combine sauce ingredients in a bowl.
2. Refrigerate until ready to use.
3. Mix the ingredients for the patties in a bowl.
4. Form patties from this mixture.
5. Preheat your air fryer to 350 degrees F.
6. Cook the patties for 15 minutes.
7. Serve with the sauce.

Serving Suggestion:

Garnish with lemon wedges.

Tip:

You can also use canned salmon flakes for this recipe.

Nutritional Information Per Serving:

Calories: 351
Total Fat: 30.2g
Saturated Fat: 5.0g
Cholesterol: 52mg
Sodium: 568mg
Potassium: 317mg
Total Carbohydrates: 6.1g
Dietary Fiber: 1.4g
Protein: 15.6g
Sugars: 0g

Breaded Shrimp

Serves: 4
Preparation and Cooking Time: 40 minutes

Ingredients:

Sauce:
1 tablespoon hot sauce
1/4 cup sweet chili sauce
1/2 cup light mayonnaise
Shrimp:
1 lb. shrimp, peeled and deveined
1 egg, beaten
1 cup breadcrumbs

Preparation:

1. Blend hot sauce, sweet chilli sauce and mayo in a bowl.
2. Cover and refrigerate.
3. Dip the shrimp in egg and then cover with breadcrumbs.
4. Add to the Ninja air fryer basket.
5. Cook at 350 degrees F for 12 minutes or until golden and crispy.
6. Serve with the spicy sauce.

Serving Suggestion:

Serve on top of large lettuce leaves.

Nutritional Information Per Serving:

Calories: 415
Total Fat: 23.9g
Saturated Fat: 4.0g
Cholesterol: 183mg
Sodium: 894mg
Total Carbohydrates: 32.7g
Dietary Fiber: 1.7g
Protein: 23.9g
Sugars: 3g

Roasted Cauliflower & Broccoli

Serves: 6
Preparation and Cooking Time: 25 minutes

Ingredients:

2 tablespoons olive oil
1/4 teaspoon paprika
1/2 teaspoon garlic powder
Salt and pepper to taste
3 cups cauliflower florets
3 cups broccoli florets, steamed

Preparation:

1. Preheat your air fryer to 400 degrees F.
2. Mix the oil, paprika, garlic powder, salt and pepper in a bowl.
3. Toss the veggies in the mixture.
4. Cook for 10 to 12 minutes, shaking once or twice.

Serving Suggestion:

Serve with cooked brown rice or as side dish to main course.

Tip:

Don't forget to shake the air fryer basket to ensure even cooking of the vegetables.

Nutritional Information Per Serving:

Calories: 68
Total fat: 4.7g
Saturated fat: 0.6g
Cholesterol: 0mg
Sodium: 103mg
Potassium: 297mg
Carbohydrates: 5.8g
Fiber: 2.5g
Protein: 2.3g
Sugar: 2g

Garlic Cheese Bread

Serves: 2
Preparation and Cooking Time: 15 minutes

Ingredients:

1 egg, beaten
1/4 cup Parmesan cheese, grated
1 cup mozzarella cheese, shredded
1/2 teaspoon garlic powder

Preparation:

1. Cover the air fryer basket with parchment paper.
2. Mix all the ingredients in a bowl.
3. Form a round shape from the mixture.
4. Add to the air fryer basket.
5. Cook for 10 minutes.

Serving Suggestion:

Serve warm but not too hot.

Tip:

This recipe is low carb and ideal for keto dieters.

Nutritional Information Per Serving:

Calories: 225
Total Fat: 14.3g
Saturated Fat: 8.0g
Cholesterol: 138mg
Sodium: 538mg
Potassium: 101mg
Total Carbohydrates: 2.7g
Dietary Fiber: 0.1g
Protein: 20.8g
Sugars: 1g

Buttermilk Fried Chicken

Serves: 4
Preparation and Cooking Time: 35 minutes

Ingredients:

1/2 teaspoon hot sauce
1 cup buttermilk
1/2 teaspoon garlic salt
1/4 cup tapioca flour
Salt and pepper to taste
1 egg, beaten
1/2 cup all-purpose flour
1-1/2 teaspoons brown sugar
1/2 teaspoon onion powder
1 teaspoon garlic powder
1/2 teaspoon paprika
1/4 teaspoon oregano
1 lb. chicken thighs

Preparation:

1. Mix hot sauce and milk in a plate.
2. Combine the garlic salt, tapioca flour, salt and pepper in another dish.
3. Transfer the egg to a bowl.
4. Blend the rest of the ingredients except the chicken.
5. Dip each chicken in the milk mixture, tapioca mixture, egg and seasoned flour. Cook in the air fryer at 380 degrees F for 10 minutes.
6. Turn and cook for another 10 minutes.

Serving Suggestion:

Serve with mashed potatoes and gravy or steamed veggies.

Tip:

Use chicken thigh fillet.

Nutritional Information Per Serving:

Calories: 335
Total fat: 13.6g
Saturated fat: 4g
Cholesterol: 114mg
Sodium: 1550mg
Potassium: 320mg
Carbohydrates: 27.4g
Fiber: 0.7g
Sugar: 5g
Protein: 24.3g

Chapter 4: 20 Red Meat Recipes

Meatloaf

Serves: 4
Preparation and Cooking Time: 45 minutes

Ingredients:

- 1 lb. lean ground beef
- 1 onion, chopped
- 3 tablespoons bread crumbs
- 1 egg, beaten
- Salt and pepper to taste
- 1 tablespoon thyme, chopped
- 2 mushrooms, sliced
- 1 tablespoon olive oil

Preparation:

1. Combine all the ingredients except the oil.
2. Mix well.
3. Transfer mixture to a loaf pan.
4. Brush top with oil.
5. Add to the air fryer basket.
6. Cook at 350 degrees F for 25 to 30 minutes.

Serving Suggestion:

Let rest for 10 minutes before slicing and serving.

Tip:

You can also press mushrooms on top of the meatloaf before cooking instead of adding it to the mixture.

Nutritional Information Per Serving:

Calories: 297
Total Fat: 18.8g
Saturated Fat: 6.0g
Cholesterol: 126mg
Sodium: 706mg
Potassium: 361mg
Total Carbohydrates: 5.9g
Dietary Fiber: 0.8g
Protein: 24.8g
Sugars: 1g

Tender & Juicy Pork Chops

Serves: 4
Preparation and Cooking Time: 35 minutes

Ingredients:

- 4 pork chops
- 2 tablespoons olive oil
- 1 teaspoon paprika
- 1/2 cup Parmesan cheese, grated
- 1 teaspoon garlic powder
- 1 teaspoon dried parsley
- Salt and pepper to taste

Preparation:

1. Preheat your air fryer to 380 degrees F.
2. Brush both sides of the pork chops with oil.
3. Mix the rest of the ingredients.

4. Dredge each of the pork chop with this mixture.
5. Cook in the air fryer for 10 minutes.

Serving Suggestion:

Sprinkle with chopped parsley.

Tip:

Use boneless pork chops for this recipe.

Nutritional Information Per Serving:

Calories: 305
Total Fat: 16.6g
Saturated Fat: 5.0g
Cholesterol: 90mg
Sodium: 685mg
Potassium: 457mg
Total Carbohydrates: 1.5g
Dietary Fiber: 0.4g
Protein: 35.3g
Sugars: 0g

Steak & Mushrooms

Serves: 4
Preparation and Cooking Time: 4 hours and 50 minutes

Ingredients:

- 1 lb. beef sirloin steak, sliced into cubes
- 8 oz. mushrooms, sliced
- 1/4 cup Worcestershire sauce
- 1 tablespoon olive oil
- 1 teaspoon dried parsley
- 1 teaspoon paprika
- 1 teaspoon crushed chili flakes

Preparation:

1. Mix all the ingredients in a bowl.
2. Cover and marinate in the refrigerator for 4 hours.
3. Preheat your Ninja air fryer to 400 degrees F.
4. Add the steak and mushrooms without the marinade in the air fryer.
5. Cook for 5 minutes.
6. Shake and cook for another 5 minutes.

Serving Suggestion:

Serve with roasted broccoli.

Tip:

You can also slice the beef into strips.

Nutritional Information Per Serving:

Calories: 225
Total Fat: 13.2g
Saturated Fat: 4.0g
Cholesterol: 60mg
Sodium: 213mg
Potassium: 590mg
Total Carbohydrates: 5.8g
Dietary Fiber: 0.9g
Protein: 20.8g
Sugars: 3g

Rib Eye Steak

Serves: 2
Preparation and Cooking Time: 2 hours and 25 minutes

Ingredients:

- 2 rib eye steaks
- 1/4 cup olive oil
- 1/2 cup soy sauce
- 4 teaspoons steak seasoning

Preparation:

1. Marinate the steaks in the mixture of oil, soy sauce and steak seasoning for at least 2 hours.
2. Preheat your air fryer to 400 degrees F.
3. Cook the steaks for 7 minutes.
4. Flip and cook for another 8 minutes.

Serving Suggestion:

Serve with green salad or mashed potatoes.

Tip:

Marinate in the morning and cook in the evening.

Nutritional Information Per Serving:

Calories: 652
Total Fat: 49.1g
Saturated Fat: 12.0g
Cholesterol: 165mg
Sodium: 4044mg
Potassium: 661mg
Total Carbohydrates: 7.5g
Dietary Fiber: 0.7g
Protein: 44g
Sugars: 1g

Pizza Hot Dogs

Serves: 2
Preparation and Cooking Time: 15 minutes

Ingredients:

2 hot dogs
4 slices pepperoni
1/2 cup tomato sauce
2 hot dog buns, sliced in half
2 teaspoons black olives, sliced
1/4 cup mozzarella cheese, shredded

Preparation:

1. Preheat your air fryer to 390 degrees F.
2. Add the hot dogs to the air fryer basket.
3. Cook for 3 minutes.
4. Slice in half.
5. Spread the tomato sauce on top of the hot dog buns.
6. Top with the sliced hot dogs, pepperoni, olives and cheese.
7. Cook in the air fryer for 2 minutes.

Tip:

You can also use pizza sauce.

Nutritional Information Per Serving:

Calories: 444
Total Fat: 28.2g
Saturated Fat: 11.0g
Cholesterol: 57mg
Sodium: 1408mg
Potassium: 172mg
Total Carbohydrates: 28.6g
Dietary Fiber: 2g
Protein: 18.1g
Sugars: 6g

Baby Back Ribs

Serves: 4
Preparation and Cooking Time: 1 hour and 20 minutes

Ingredients:

- 1 rack baby back ribs, sliced into 4
- 1 tablespoon liquid smoke flavoring
- 1 tablespoon olive oil
- 1/2 teaspoon chili powder
- 1/2 teaspoon onion powder
- 1/2 teaspoon garlic powder
- Salt and pepper to taste
- 1 tablespoon brown sugar
- 1 cup barbecue sauce

Preparation:

1. Combine liquid smoke and oil.
2. Brush both sides of rack with the mixture.
3. In a bowl, mix the rest of the ingredients except the barbecue sauce.
4. Season rack with the mixture.
5. Marinate for 30 minutes.
6. Preheat your air fryer to 375 degrees F.
7. Add the ribs to the air fryer basket.
8. Cook for 15 minutes.
9. Flip and cook for another 10 minutes.
10. Brush with barbecue sauce and cook for another 5 minutes.

Serving Suggestion:

Serve with grilled asparagus spears or corn cobs.

Tip:

Cook in batches and do not overcrowd.

Nutritional Information Per Serving:

Calories: 445
Total Fat: 29g
Saturated Fat: 9.0g
Cholesterol: 88mg
Sodium: 1070mg
Potassium: 384mg
Total Carbohydrates: 26.8g
Dietary Fiber: 0.6g
Protein: 18.2g
Sugars: 20g

Meatballs in Tomato Sauce

Serves: 4
Preparation and Cooking Time: 18 minutes

Ingredients:

- 1 onion, chopped
- 20 oz. minced beef
- 1 tablespoon parsley, chopped
- 1 teaspoon dried thyme
- 1 egg, beaten
- 3 tablespoons breadcrumbs
- Salt and pepper to taste
- 3/4 cup tomato sauce

Preparation:

1. Add all the ingredients in a bowl.
2. Form balls from the mixture.
3. Preheat your Ninja air fryer to 400 degrees F.
4. Cook the meatballs for 7 minutes.
5. Transfer to a small baking pan.
6. Pour in the tomato sauce.
7. Put it back to the air fryer.
8. Cook for another 5 minutes.

Serving Suggestion:

Garnish with parsley.

Tip:

You can also serve the meatballs without the tomato sauce.

Nutritional Information Per Serving:

Calories: 233
Total Fat: 13.5g
Saturated Fat: 5.0g
Cholesterol: 87mg
Sodium: 277mg
Potassium: 325mg
Total Carbohydrates: 12.1g
Dietary Fiber: 1.9g
Protein: 15.1g
Sugars: 5g

Ranch Pork Chops

Serves: 4
Preparation and Cooking Time: 25 minutes

Ingredients:

- Cooking spray
- 4 pork chops
- 2 teaspoons ranch salad dressing mix

Preparation:

1. Spray pork chops with oil.
2. Seasons with the dressing powder.
3. Preheat your air fryer to 390 degrees F.
4. Add the chops to the preheated air fryer.
5. Cook for 5 minutes. Flip and cook for another 5 minutes.

Serving Suggestion:

Serve with green salad.

Tip:

Reduce cooking time for thin cut pork chops.

Nutritional Information Per Serving:

Calories: 260
Total Fat: 9.1g
Saturated Fat: 3.0g
Cholesterol: 107mg
Sodium: 148mg
Potassium: 549mg
Total Carbohydrates: 0.6g
Dietary Fiber: 0g
Protein: 40.8g
Sugars: 0g

Cajun Pork Chops

Serves: 4
Preparation and Cooking Time: 20 minutes

Ingredients:

- 4 pork chops
- 1 teaspoon Cajun seasoning
- 2 eggs, beaten
- 1-1/2 cups croutons, crushed
- Cooking spray

Preparation:

1. Preheat your air fryer to 390 degrees F.
2. Season both sides of the pork chops with Cajun seasoning.
3. Dip the pork chops in egg.
4. Dredge them in croutons.
5. Spray both sides with oil.
6. Cook in the air fryer for 5 minutes.
7. Flip and cook for another 5 minutes.

Serving Suggestion:

Garnish with orange slices.

Tip:

Use boneless pork chops.

Nutritional Information Per Serving:

Calories: 394
Total Fat: 18.1g
Saturated Fat: 6.0g
Cholesterol: 218mg
Sodium: 429mg
Potassium: 758mg
Total Carbohydrates: 10g
Dietary Fiber: 0.8g
Protein: 44.7g
Sugars: 1g

Steak Strips with Mushrooms

Serves: 2
Preparation and Cooking Time: 30 minutes

Ingredients:

- 1/4 cup olive oil
- 1/2 teaspoon garlic powder
- 2 teaspoons steak seasoning
- 1 tablespoon soy sauce
- 2 steaks, sliced into strips
- 4 oz. mushrooms

Preparation:

1. In a bowl, mix the oil, garlic powder, seasoning and soy sauce.
2. Marinate the steak strips for 15 minutes.
3. Preheat your air fryer to 390 degrees F.
4. Cook the steak and mushrooms in the air fryer basket for 5 minutes.
5. Shake and cook for another 5 minutes.

Serving Suggestion:

Serve on top of mashed potatoes or brown rice.

Tip:

Use garlic salt if garlic powder is not available.

Nutritional Information Per Serving:

Calories: 548
Total Fat: 40.1g
Saturated Fat: 9.0g
Cholesterol: 98mg
Sodium: 731mg
Potassium: 777mg
Total Carbohydrates: 4.9g
Dietary Fiber: 0.9g
Protein: 41g
Sugars: 1g

Spring Rolls

Serves: 20
Preparation and Cooking Time: 55 minutes

Ingredients:

- 1 tablespoon sesame oil
- 1 onion, diced
- 3 cloves garlic, crushed and minced
- 7 oz. lean ground beef
- 1/4 cup frozen mixed veggies
- 2 oz. rice noodles, soaked in water for 5 minutes
- 1 teaspoon soy sauce
- 16 oz. egg roll wrappers
- 1 tablespoon vegetable oil

Preparation:

1. Pour the oil in a pan over medium heat.
2. Add the onion, garlic, ground beef and mixed veggies.
3. Cook for 6 minutes.
4. Add the noodles and soy sauce.
5. Remove from heat.
6. Let sit for 5 minutes and then drain.
7. Preheat your Ninja air fryer to 350 degrees F>
8. Add the filling on top of the egg roll wrappers.
9. Roll and seal.
10. Brush with the vegetable oil.
11. Cook in the air fryer for 8 minutes or until crispy.

Serving Suggestion:

Serve with lettuce leaves on the side.

Tip:

You can also use fresh mixed vegetables.

Nutritional Information Per Serving:

Calories: 112
Total Fat: 3.2g
Saturated Fat: 1.0g
Cholesterol: 8mg
Sodium: 155mg
Potassium: 52mg
Total Carbohydrates: 16.4g
Dietary Fiber: 0.7g
Protein: 4.1g
Sugars: 0g

Pineapple Pork

Serves: 4
Preparation and Cooking Time: 40 minutes

Ingredients:

- 16 oz. pork loin, sliced into cubes
- Salt and pepper to taste
- 1 clove garlic, crushed and minced
- 1 teaspoon ginger, minced
- 1 green pepper, sliced into cubes
- 1/2 pineapple, sliced into cubes
- 1 tablespoon brown sugar
- 2 tablespoons soy sauce

- 1 teaspoon vegetable oil

1. Preparation:

2. Season the pork cubes with salt and pepper.
3. Add these to the air fryer basket along with the garlic, ginger, pepper, and pineapple. Mix well.
4. In a bowl, mix the sugar, soy sauce and oil.
5. Pour this over the ingredients.
6. Cook in the air fryer for 20 minutes.

Serving Suggestion:

Garnish with sesame seeds.

Tip:

You can also use canned pineapple chunks.

Nutritional Information Per Serving:

Calories: 372
Total Fat: 18.3g
Saturated Fat: 6.0g
Cholesterol: 71mg
Sodium: 806mg
Potassium: 711mg
Total Carbohydrates: 28.6g
Dietary Fiber: 3.3g
Protein: 24.4g
Sugars: 21g

Pork Skewers

Serves: 4
Preparation and Cooking Time: 40 minutes

Ingredients:

- 1 lb. pork tenderloin, sliced into cubes
- 1 tablespoon vegetable oil
- 5 teaspoons onion powder
- 1 tablespoon ground allspice
- 2 tablespoons sugar
- 5 teaspoons thyme
- 1/4 teaspoon ground cloves
- 3/4 teaspoon ground nutmeg
- Salt and pepper to taste

Preparation:

1. Preheat your air fryer to 350 degrees F.
2. Thread the pork cubes into skewers.
3. Brush both sides with oil.
4. In a bowl, mix the rest of the ingredients.
5. Season both sides with this mixture.
6. Cook in the air fryer for 6 to 8 minutes.

Serving Suggestion:

Serve with salsa or garlic sauce.

Tip:

Add cayenne pepper to make the dish spicy.

Nutritional Information Per Serving:

Calories: 313
Total Fat: 10.8g
Saturated Fat: 5.0g
Cholesterol: 49mg
Sodium: 1268mg
Potassium: 656mg
Total Carbohydrates: 34.6g
Dietary Fiber: 7.4g
Protein: 22.3g
Sugars: 18g

Pork Meatballs

Serves: 12

Preparation and Cooking Time: 35 minutes

Ingredients:

- 12 oz. ground pork
- 8 oz. ground sausage
- 1 egg, beaten
- 1/2 cup breadcrumbs
- 1/2 teaspoon paprika
- 1 teaspoon dried parsley
- Salt and pepper to taste

Preparation:

1. Preheat your air fryer to 350 degrees F.
2. Mix all the ingredients in a bowl.
3. Add to the air fryer basket.
4. Cook for 2 minutes.
5. Shake and cook for another 3 minutes.
6. Shake once more and cook for 5 more minutes.

Serving Suggestion:

Serve with corn salsa.

Tip:

You can use cayenne pepper in place of paprika.

Nutritional Information Per Serving:

Calories: 120
Total Fat: 8.1g
Saturated Fat: 3.0g
Cholesterol: 41mg
Sodium: 391mg
Potassium: 119mg
Total Carbohydrates: 3.8g
Dietary Fiber: 0.1g
Protein: 8.5g
Sugars: 0g

Bratwurst Bites

Serves: 6

Preparation and Cooking Time: 40 minutes

Ingredients:

- 1/2 cup mustard
- 3 tablespoons honey
- 1/2 cup dark beer
- 1/2 teaspoon ground turmeric
- 5 links bratwurst, sliced
- 6 sweet peppers, minced

Preparation:

1. Combine all the ingredients except the last two in a saucepan.
2. Cook over medium heat for 3 minutes, stirring frequently.
3. Add the sausages and peppers in the air fryer basket.
4. Mix well.
5. Cook at 400 degrees F for 5 minutes.
6. Shake and cook for another 5 minutes.
7. Serve with the mustard sauce.

Serving Suggestion:

Serve with green salad.

Tip:

You can also use other types of sausages like

cervelat.

Nutritional Information Per Serving:

Calories: 112
Total Fat: 3.3g
Saturated Fat: 1.0g

Cholesterol: 16mg
Sodium: 324mg
Potassium: 49mg
Total Carbohydrates: 15.2g
Dietary Fiber: 0.4g
Protein: 3.6g
Sugars: 9g

Burgers

Serves: 2
Preparation and Cooking Time: 25 minutes

Ingredients:

- Cooking spray
- 2 tablespoons olive oil
- 8 oz. lean ground beef
- 1/2 teaspoon red pepper flakes
- 2 teaspoons fresh oregano, chopped
- 2 garlic cloves, grated
- Salt to taste
- 1/4 cup onion, sliced thinly
- 1/2 cup spinach
- 1/2 tablespoon red-wine vinegar
- 2 burger buns

Preparation:

1. Spray the air fryer basket with oil.
2. Mix the oil, beef, red pepper flakes, oregano, garlic and salt in a bowl.
3. Form into patties.
4. Cook in the air fryer at 360 degrees F for 15 minutes, flipping halfway through.
5. Toss the onion, spinach in vinegar.
6. Serve the burger in burger buns with the onion and spinach mixture.

Serving Suggestion:

Serve with feta cheese.

Nutritional Information Per Serving:

Calories: 351
Total Fat: 15.6g
Saturated Fat: 5.7g
Cholesterol: 101mg
Sodium: 777mg
Potassium: 420mg
Total Carbohydrates: 26g
Dietary Fiber: 4g
Protein: 28.4g
Sugars: 5g

Peppers Stuffed with Beef

Serves: 3
Preparation and Cooking Time: 30 minutes

Ingredients:

- Cooking spray
- 3 large bell peppers
- 1 tablespoon olive oil

- 12 oz. ground beef
- 1/2 cup cooked brown rice
- 1/4 cup breadcrumbs
- 3 tablespoons parsley, chopped
- 3/4 cup marinara sauce
- 1/4 cup Parmesan cheese, grated
- Salt and pepper to taste
- 1/4 cup mozzarella cheese, shredded

Preparation:

1. Spray the air fryer basket with oil.
2. Slice the tops off the red bell peppers.
3. Pour the oil in a pan over medium heat.
4. Cook the turkey, rice and breadcrumbs for 5 minutes, stirring frequently.
5. Add the rest of the ingredients except mozzarella cheese.
6. Pour mixture into the bell peppers.
7. Add the bell peppers to the air fryer.
8. Cook at 350 degrees F for 8 minutes.
9. Sprinkle top with mozzarella.
10. Cook for 2 minutes.

Tip:

You can also use ground turkey in place of ground beef.

Nutritional Information Per Serving:

Calories: 407
Total Fat: 20.6g
Saturated Fat: 5.3g
Cholesterol: 96mg
Sodium: 340mg
Potassium: 575mg
Total Carbohydrates: 25.6g
Dietary Fiber: 1g
Protein: 29.3g
Sugars: 7g

Crispy Pork Chops

Serves: 2
Preparation and Cooking Time: 30 minutes

Ingredients:

- 1/4 teaspoon onion powder
- 1/4 teaspoon garlic powder
- 1/2 cup panko breadcrumbs
- 1 teaspoon paprika
- 2 pork chops
- Cooking spray
- Salt to taste

Preparation:

1. Mix the onion powder, garlic powder, breadcrumbs and paprika in a bowl.
2. Coat the pork with the mixture.
3. Spray the air fryer basket with oil.
4. Cook the pork in the air fryer at 360 degrees F for 15 minutes, turning once halfway through.
5. Season with salt before serving.

Serving Suggestion:

Serve with roasted vegetables.

Tip:

Let rest for 5 minutes before slicing.

Nutritional Information Per Serving:

Calories: 230
Total Fat: 6.4g
Saturated Fat: 1.9g

Cholesterol: 72mg
Sodium: 372mg
Potassium: 338mg
Total Carbohydrates: 16.1g

Dietary Fiber: 1g
Protein: 25.1g
Sugars: 1g

Pork Nuggets

Serves: 2
Preparation and Cooking Time: 40 minutes

Ingredients:

- Cooking spray
- 1 tablespoon confectioners' sugar
- Salt and pepper to taste
- 1/4 teaspoon garlic powder
- 1/4 cup cornstarch
- 1/4 cup buttermilk
- 1-1/2 cup crushed cornflakes
- 8 oz. pork tenderloin, sliced

Preparation:

1. Spray the air fryer basket with oil.
2. Mix the sugar, salt, pepper, garlic powder and cornstarch in a bowl.
3. Pour the milk in another bowl.
4. Place the cornflakes in another dish.
5. Coat the pork with the cornstarch mixture.
6. Dip in milk and then dredge with cornflakes.
7. Cook in the air fryer at 400 degrees F for up to 10 minutes or until golden.

Serving Suggestion:

Serve with bread, rice or salad.

Nutritional Information Per Serving:

Calories: 319
Total Fat: 3.8g
Saturated Fat: 1.4g
Cholesterol: 66mg
Sodium: 535mg
Potassium: 287mg
Total Carbohydrates: 44.2g
Dietary Fiber: 1.2g
Protein: 26.1g
Sugars: 8g

Lamb Meatballs

Serves: 2
Preparation and Cooking Time: 20 minutes

Ingredients:

- Cooking spray
- 10 oz. ground lamb
- 1/4 cup breadcrumbs
- 3 tablespoons cilantro, chopped
- 2 tablespoons sweet chili sauce
- 2 tablespoons mayonnaise
- 1 egg, beaten
- Salt and pepper to taste

Preparation:

1. Spray air fryer basket with oil.
2. Mix all the ingredients.

3. Form meatballs from the mixture.
4. Cook in the air fryer at 400 degrees F for 10 minutes, shaking halfway through.

Serving Suggestion:

Serve with chilli sauce

Nutritional Information Per Serving:

Calories: 399

Total Fat: 15.5g
Saturated Fat: 2.1g
Cholesterol: 150mg
Sodium: 537mg
Potassium: 731mg
Total Carbohydrates: 27.9g
Dietary Fiber: 2.8g
Protein: 34.6g
Sugars: 10g

Chapter 5: 20 Poultry Recipes

Chicken Tenderloins

Serves: 4
Preparation and Cooking Time: 30 minutes

Ingredients:

- 2 tablespoons vegetable oil
- 1/2 cup dry bread crumbs
- 8 chicken tenderloins
- 1 egg, beaten

Preparation:

1. Preheat your air fryer to 350 degrees F.
2. Mix the oil and breadcrumbs.
3. Dip the chicken in egg and then coat with the breadcrumb mixture.
4. Cook in the air fryer for 12 minutes.

Serving Suggestion:

Garnish with lemon wedges.

Tip:

You can replace oil with butter.

Nutritional Information Per Serving:

Calories: 253
Total fat: 11.4g
Saturated fat: 2.4g
Cholesterol: 109mg
Sodium: 171mg
Potassium: 231mg
Carbohydrates: 9.8g
Fiber: 0.6g
Sugar: 1g
Protein: 26.2g

Crispy Chicken Thighs

Serves: 4
Preparation and Cooking Time: 30 minutes

Ingredients:

- 4 chicken thighs
- 2 teaspoons olive oil
- Salt and pepper to taste
- 3/4 teaspoon garlic powder
- 1 teaspoon smoked paprika

Preparation:

1. Preheat your air fryer to 400 degrees F.
2. Brush both sides of the chicken with oil.
3. Season with the salt, pepper, garlic powder and paprika.
4. Cook in the air fryer for 20 minutes, flipping halfway through.

Serving Suggestion:

Serve with potato fries.

Tip:

Cook with skin on.

Nutritional Information Per Serving:

Calories: 213
Total fat: 14.2g
Saturated fat: 3.6g
Cholesterol: 71mg
Sodium: 355mg

Potassium: 192mg
Carbohydrates: 0.9g
Fiber: 0.3g

Sugar: 0g
Protein: 19.3g

Garlic Chicken

Serves: 4
Preparation and Cooking Time: 2 hours and 35 minutes

Ingredients:

- 2 tablespoons olive oil
- 1/4 cup lemon juice
- 2 cloves garlic, minced
- Salt and pepper to taste
- 1 teaspoon Dijon mustard
- 4 chicken thighs

Preparation:

1. Mix the oil, juice, garlic, salt, pepper and mustard in a bowl.
2. Cover and marinate the chicken in this mixture for 2 hours in the refrigerator.
3. Preheat your air fryer to 360 degrees F. Cook in the air fryer for 20 to 25 minutes.

Serving Suggestion:

Serve with cauliflower rice.

Nutritional Information Per Serving:

Calories: 258
Total fat: 18.6g
Saturated fat: 4.2g
Cholesterol: 71mg
Sodium: 242mg
Potassium: 215mg
Carbohydrates: 3.6g
Fiber: 0.7g
Protein: 19.4g
Sugar: 0g

Buffalo Chicken Breast

Serves: 4
Preparation and Cooking Time: 35 minutes

Ingredients:

- 1 egg, beaten
- 1 tablespoon hot sauce
- 1/2 cup Greek yogurt
- 1 tablespoon garlic pepper seasoning
- 1 tablespoon sweet paprika
- 1 tablespoon cayenne pepper
- 1 cup panko bread crumbs
- 1 lb. chicken breast, sliced into strips

Preparation:

1. Mix the egg, hot sauce and yogurt in a bowl.
2. In another bowl, blend the peppers and breadcrumbs.
3. Dip each chicken strip in the first bowl.
4. Coat with the seasoned breadcrumbs.
5. Place the chicken strips in the air fryer basket.
6. Cook at 350 degrees F for 8 minutes.
7. Flip and cook for another 7 minutes.

Serving Suggestion:

Serve with blue cheese dressing.

Tip:

Cook in batches and do not overcrowd.

Nutritional Information Per Serving:

Calories: 234
Total Fat: 4.6g
Saturated Fat: 1.0g
Cholesterol: 65mg
Sodium: 696mg
Potassium: 325mg
Total Carbohydrates: 22.1g
Dietary Fiber: 1.1g
Protein: 31.2g
Sugars: 2g

Chicken Wrapped with Bacon

Serves: 4
Preparation and Cooking Time: 2 hours and 35 minutes

Ingredients:

- 1/2 stick butter, softened
- Salt and pepper to taste
- 1/2 clove garlic, minced
- 1/4 teaspoon dried basil
- 1/4 teaspoon dried thyme
- 1/4 lb. bacon thick slices
- 1 lb. chicken thigh fillets, sliced
- 2 teaspoons garlic, crushed and minced

Preparation:

1. Mix the butter, salt, pepper, garlic, basil and thyme in a bowl.
2. Add the mixture on a wax paper.
3. Roll and refrigerate for 2 hours.
4. Add the bacon on a wax paper sheet.
5. Add the chicken on top of the bacon.
6. Sprinkle with the minced garlic.
7. Place the butter roll in the middle.
8. Roll the bacon and secure.
9. Transfer to the air fryer.
10. Cook at 370 degrees F for 25 minutes.

Serving Suggestion:

Serve as appetizer.

Nutritional Information Per Serving:

Calories: 453
Total fat: 34.3g
Saturated fat: 13.9g
Cholesterol: 150mg
Sodium: 441mg
Potassium: 340mg
Carbohydrates: 1g
Fiber: 0.2g
Protein: 33.4g
Sugars: 0g

Chicken Nuggets

Serves: 8
Preparation and Cooking Time: 30 minutes

Ingredients:

- 1 cup buttermilk
- 2 lb. chicken tenderloin, sliced
- 1 cup flour
- 3 tablespoons Parmesan cheese, grated
- Salt and pepper to taste
- 1 tablespoon parsley flakes
- 1 tablespoon paprika
- 2 eggs, beaten

- 2 cups breadcrumbs
- Cooking spray

Preparation:

1. Soak the chicken in buttermilk.
2. Meanwhile, mix the flour, cheese, salt, pepper, parsley and paprika.
3. Add the eggs in another bowl.
4. Place the breadcrumbs in a dish.
5. Coat the chicken in the flour mixture, in the eggs and then in the breadcrumbs.
6. Preheat your Ninja air fryer to 400 degrees F.
7. Spray the air fryer basket with oil.
8. Add the nuggets to the basket.
9. Cook for 10 minutes.
10. Turn and cook for another 5 minutes or until crispy.

Serving Suggestion:

Serve with sunny side up eggs.

Tip:

Shake to ensure even cooking.

Nutritional Information Per Serving:

Calories: 310
Total Fat: 6.8g
Saturated Fat: 2.0g
Cholesterol: 119mg
Sodium: 564mg
Potassium: 315mg
Total Carbohydrates: 33.5g
Dietary Fiber: 0.9g
Protein: 33.4g
Sugars: 2g

Herbed Crispy Chicken

Serves: 4
Preparation and Cooking Time: 35 minutes

Ingredients:

- 1 lb. chicken thigh fillets, sliced into strips
- 1/4 teaspoon dried basil
- 1/4 teaspoon dried rosemary
- Garlic salt to taste
- 1 cup breadcrumbs
- 1/4 cup flour
- 1 egg

Preparation:

1. Preheat your air fryer to 380 degrees F.
2. Season chicken with basil and rosemary.
3. Mix the garlic salt and breadcrumbs.
4. Dip the chicken in flour, egg and then in the garlic salt mixture.
5. Cook in the air fryer for 10 minutes.
6. Flip and cook for another 5 minutes.

Serving Suggestion:

Garnish with lime wedges.

Tip:

You can also spread chicken with butter before adding herbs.

Nutritional Information Per Serving:

Calories: 335
Total fat: 13.6g
Saturated fat: 4g
Cholesterol: 114mg
Sodium: 1550mg
Potassium: 320mg
Carbohydrates: 27.4g
Fiber: 0.7g 3 %

Protein: 24.3g   Sugars: 5g

Mexican Chicken

Serves: 2
Preparation and Cooking Time: 30 minutes

Ingredients:

- 1 chicken breast fillet
- 4 teaspoons ground cumin
- 4 teaspoons chili powder
- 2 teaspoons chipotle flakes
- 2 teaspoons Mexican oregano
- Salt and pepper to taste
- 1 red bell pepper, sliced into strips
- 1 onion, sliced thinly
- 2 teaspoons oil

Preparation:

1. Preheat your Ninja air fryer to 400 degrees F.
2. Flatten the chicken with a meat mallet.
3. Mix all the spices, salt and pepper.
4. Season both sides of the chicken with this mixture.
5. Add the onion and red bell pepper strips on top of the chicken.
6. Roll and secure with a toothpick.
7. Drizzle with oil.
8. Cook in the air fryer for 6 minutes.
9. Turn and cook for another 5 minutes.

Serving Suggestion:

Drizzle with lime juice. Serve with tortillas.

Tip:

You can also use turkey fillet.

Nutritional Information Per Serving:

Calories: 185
Total fat: 8.5g
Saturated fat: 1.3g
Cholesterol: 32mg
Sodium: 171mg
Potassium: 499mg
Carbohydrates: 15.2g
Fiber: 5.4g
Sugar: 5g
Protein: 14.8g

Roasted Turkey

Serves: 6
Preparation and Cooking Time: 8 hours and 50 minutes

Ingredients:

- 2 cups water
- 1/4 cup salt
- 1/4 cup brown sugar
- 3 lb. turkey breast
- 3 tablespoons butter
- Salt and pepper to taste

Preparation:

1. Add water to a pot and bring to a boil.
2. Add salt, pepper and brown sugar.
3. Let the mixture cool.
4. Transfer to a large container.
5. Soak the turkey in the brine for 8 hours in

the refrigerator.

6. Preheat your air fryer to 390 degrees F.
7. Dry the turkey.
8. Sprinkle with salt and pepper.
9. Cook the turkey for 15 minutes.
10. Lower temperature to 360 degrees F and cook for another 15 minutes.
11. Turn and cook for another 5 minutes.
12. Increase the temperature to 390 degrees F.
13. Cook for 15 minutes more.

Serving Suggestion:

Serve with vegetable side dish.

Tip:

Spray turkey with oil halfway through the cooking.

Nutritional Information Per Serving:

Calories: 348
Total Fat: 5.3g
Saturated Fat: 3.0g
Cholesterol: 174mg
Sodium: 174mg
Potassium: 598mg
Total Carbohydrates: 12.1g
Dietary Fiber: 0g
Protein: 59.4g
Sugars: 12g

Buffalo Chicken Wings

Serves: 4
Preparation and Cooking Time: 1 hour and 5 minutes

Ingredients:

- 2-1/2 lb. chicken wings
- 1 tablespoon olive oil
- 1/4 cup hot sauce
- 2 tablespoons vinegar
- 1/2 cup butter
- 1/4 teaspoon cayenne pepper
- 1 teaspoon garlic powder

Preparation:

1. Preheat your air fryer to 360 degrees F.
2. Add the chicken wings to a bowl.
3. Toss in oil.
4. Cook in the air fryer for 25 minutes.
5. Flip and cook for another 5 minutes.
6. Mix the rest of the ingredients in another bowl.
7. Pour the sauce over the wings and coat evenly.

Serving Suggestion:

Garnish with chopped parsley on top.

Nutritional Information Per Serving:

Calories: 481
Total fat: 41.5g
Saturated fat: 18.9g
Cholesterol: 120mg
Sodium: 1328mg
Potassium: 147mg
Carbohydrates: 7.3g
Fiber: 0.1g
Protein: 20.7g
Sugars: 0g

Crispy Chicken Drumsticks

Serves: 2
Preparation and Cooking Time: 30 minutes

Ingredients:

- 1 tablespoon water
- 1 egg
- 1/2 teaspoon onion powder
- 1/2 teaspoon garlic powder
- 1/2 cup crushed cornflakes
- 1/4 teaspoon paprika
- 1/4 teaspoon chili powder
- 1/4 teaspoon Cajun seasoning
- Salt to taste
- 6 chicken drumsticks
- Cooking spray

Preparation:

1. Combine the water and egg in a bowl.
2. In another bowl, mix the rest of the ingredients except the chicken.
3. Dip the chicken drumsticks in the egg mixture, and in the spice mixture.
4. Preheat your Ninja air fryer to 400 degrees F.
5. Spray the chicken with oil.
6. Cook for 10 minutes.
7. Turn and cook for another 10 minutes.

Serving Suggestion:

Serve with eggplant fries or potato fries.

Nutritional Information Per Serving:

Calories: 536
Total fat: 19.5g
Saturated fat: 5.2g
Cholesterol: 280mg
Sodium: 1126mg
Potassium: 584mg
Carbohydrates: 22.1g
Fiber: 0.5g
Protein: 64.8g
Sugars: 3g

Peruvian Chicken

Serves: 6
Preparation and Cooking Time: 30 minutes

Ingredients:

- Olive oil
- 1 tablespoon honey
- 2 cloves garlic, grated
- 1/2 teaspoon dried oregano
- 1/2 teaspoon smoked paprika
- 1 teaspoon ground cumin
- Salt and pepper to taste
- 6 chicken drumsticks

Preparation:

1. Grease your air fryer basket with oil.
2. In a bowl, mix the honey, garlic, oregano, paprika, cumin, salt and pepper.
3. Coat the chicken with the sauce.
4. Cook at 400 degrees F for 15 minutes.
5. Flip and cook for another 5 minutes.

Serving Suggestion:

Garnish with chopped cilantro.

Nutritional Information Per Serving:

Calories: 271
Total Fat: 17.7g
Saturated Fat: 7.0g
Cholesterol: 82mg

Sodium: 574mg
Potassium: 284mg
Total Carbohydrates: 5.8g
Dietary Fiber: 0.5g
Protein: 21.9g
Sugars: 3g

Popcorn Chicken

Serves: 4
Preparation and Cooking Time: 30 minutes

Ingredients:

- 1 lb. chicken breast fillet
- Salt and pepper to taste
- 1/2 teaspoon paprika
- 1/4 teaspoon ground mustard
- 1/4 teaspoon onion powder
- 1/4 teaspoon garlic powder
- 1/8 teaspoon ground thyme
- 1/8 teaspoon dried sage
- 1/8 teaspoon dried oregano
- 1/8 teaspoon dried basil
- 3 tablespoons cornstarch
- Cooking spray

Preparation:

1. Slice the chicken into smaller pieces.
2. Season the chicken with salt and pepper.
3. Combine the rest of the ingredients in a bowl.
4. Toss the chicken slices in the mixture.
5. Preheat your Ninja air fryer to 390 degrees F.
6. Spray your air fryer basket with oil.
7. Add the chicken but do not overlap.
8. Cook for 5 minutes.
9. Shake and cook for another 5 minutes.

Serving Suggestion:

Serve with gravy or ketchup.

Tip:

After coating with the cornstarch mixture, let rest for 5 minutes before cooking.

Nutritional Information Per Serving:

Calories: 152
Total fat: 2.9g
Saturated fat: 0.8g
Cholesterol: 65mg
Sodium: 493mg
Potassium: 209mg
Carbohydrates: 6.1g
Fiber: 0.3g
Protein: 23.8g
Sugars: 0g

Honey Cajun Turkey

Serves: 6
Preparation and Cooking Time: 30 minutes

Ingredients:

- 1/2 cup buttermilk
- 1 teaspoon hot sauce
- 2 lb. turkey thigh fillets
- 1/4 cup tapioca flour
- 1/4 cup all-purpose flour
- 2 teaspoons Cajun seasoning
- 1/2 teaspoon honey powder
- 1/2 teaspoon garlic salt
- 1/8 teaspoon cayenne pepper
- 1/4 teaspoon ground paprika
- 4 teaspoons honey

Preparation:

1. Mix the milk and hot sauce.
2. Marinate the turkey in this mixture for 30 minutes.
3. In a bowl, combine the flours, seasoning, garlic salt, cayenne pepper, paprika, and honey powder.
4. Dredge turkey in the flour mixture.
5. Preheat your Ninja air fryer to 360 degrees F.
6. Add the turkey to the air fryer basket.
7. Cook for 15 minutes.
8. Flip and cook for another 10 minutes.

Serving Suggestion:

Drizzle with honey before serving.

Tip:

You can also use chicken thighs for this recipe.

Nutritional Information Per Serving:

Calories: 248
Total fat: 11.5g
Saturated fat: 3.2g
Cholesterol: 65mg
Sodium: 430mg
Potassium: 187mg
Carbohydrates: 16.4g
Fiber: 0.3g
Protein: 19.1g
Sugars: 5g

Blackened Chicken

Serves: 2
Preparation and Cooking Time: 40 minutes

Ingredients:

- Salt and pepper to taste
- 2 teaspoons paprika
- 1 teaspoon cumin
- 1 teaspoon ground thyme
- 1/2 teaspoon onion powder
- 1/2 teaspoon cayenne pepper
- 2 teaspoons vegetable oil
- 24 oz. chicken breast fillets

Preparation:

1. In a bowl, mix all the ingredients except the oil and chicken.
2. Spread the mixture on a plate.
3. Brush both sides of the chicken with the oil.
4. Dredge the chicken with the spice mixture.
5. Press and marinate for 5 minutes.
6. Preheat your air fryer to 360 degrees F.
7. Cook the chicken for 10 minutes.
8. Turn and cook for another 10 minutes.

Serving Suggestion:

Serve with leafy greens or tomato salad.

Tip:

Let rest for 5 minutes before serving.

Nutritional Information Per Serving:

Calories: 432
Total fat: 9.5g
Saturated fat: 1.9g
Cholesterol: 198mg
Sodium: 516mg
Potassium: 968mg
Carbohydrates: 3.2g
Fiber: 1.5g
Protein: 79.4g
Sugars: 1g

Ranch Chicken Nuggets

Serves: 4
Preparation and Cooking Time: 40 minutes

Ingredients:

- 1 lb. chicken tenders, sliced into small pieces
- 1 oz. ranch salad dressing mix
- 2 tablespoons flour
- 1 egg, beaten
- 1 cup bread crumbs
- Cooking spray

Preparation:

1. Season both sides of chicken with ranch seasoning.
2. Marinate for 10 minutes.
3. Coat both sides with flour.
4. Dip in the egg.
5. Cover with breadcrumbs.
6. Spray the air fryer basket with oil.
7. Preheat your Ninja air fryer to 390 degrees F.
8. Cook chicken for 4 minutes.
9. Turn and cook for another 4 minutes.

Serving Suggestion:

Serve with potato fries.

Nutritional Information Per Serving:

Calories: 244
Total fat: 3.6g
Saturated fat: 1g
Cholesterol: 112mg
Sodium: 713mg
Potassium: 345mg
Carbohydrates: 25.3g
Fiber: 0.1g
Protein: 31g
Sugars: 0g

Honey Spicy Chicken Wings

Serves: 2
Preparation and Cooking Time: 40 minutes

Ingredients:

- 12 chicken wings
- Salt and garlic powder to taste
- 1 tablespoon butter
- 1 tablespoon hot pepper sauce

- 2 teaspoons rice vinegar
- 1/4 cup honey

Preparation:

1. Preheat your air fryer to 360 degrees F.
2. Season chicken wings with garlic powder and salt.
3. Add to the air fryer basket.
4. Cook for 25 minutes, shaking up to three times while cooking.
5. In a pan, melt the butter and stir in the rest of the ingredients.
6. Simmer for 10 minutes.
7. Pour the sauce over the wings and toss to coat evenly.

Serving Suggestion:

Serve with grilled corn.

Tip:

Let the chicken wings sit in the air fryer basket while simmering the sauce.

Nutritional Information Per Serving:

Calories: 586
Total fat: 32.6g
Saturated fat: 11.2g
Cholesterol: 131mg
Sodium: 1055mg
Potassium: 285mg
Carbohydrates: 36.2g
Fiber: 0.4g
Protein: 37.4g
Sugars: 35g

Korean Chicken Wings

Serves: 4
Preparation and Cooking Time: 50 minutes

Ingredients:

- Sauce:
- 2 teaspoons garlic, crushed and minced
- 1 teaspoon ginger, minced
- 3 tablespoons hot pepper paste
- 1/4 cup honey
- 1 tablespoon soy sauce
- 1 teaspoon lemon juice
- 1 tablespoon brown sugar
- 1/4 cup green onion, chopped
- Salt and pepper to taste
- Wings:
- 2 lb. chicken wings
- Salt and pepper to taste
- 1 teaspoon onion powder
- 1 teaspoon garlic powder
- 1/2 cup cornstarch

Preparation:

1. Mix all the sauce ingredients in a bowl.
2. Pour the mixture into the saucepan over medium heat.
3. Simmer for 5 minutes.
4. Remove from heat and set aside.
5. Preheat your air fryer to 400 degrees F.
6. Add the wings to a bowl and toss with the wings ingredients.
7. Cook in the air fryer for 10 minutes.
8. Shake and cook for another 10 minutes.
9. Serve with the sauce.

Serving Suggestion:

Garnish with chopped green onion and sesame seeds.

Nutritional Information Per Serving:

Calories: 346
Total fat: 11.5g
Saturated fat: 3.2g
Cholesterol: 48mg

Sodium: 1247mg
Potassium: 185mg
Carbohydrates: 44.8g
Fiber: 0.8g
Protein: 16.2g
Sugars: 24g

Herbed Fried Chicken

Serves: 6
Preparation and Cooking Time: 50 minutes

Ingredients:

- 1 tablespoon hot sauce
- 1/2 cup kefir
- 1-1/2 lb. chicken tenders
- 3 oz. Parmesan cheese, grated
- 7 oz. pork rinds, crushed
- 1/2 teaspoon smoked paprika
- 3/4 teaspoon Italian seasoning
- 1-1/2 teaspoons garlic powder

Preparation:

1. Mix hot sauce and kefir.
2. Marinate the chicken tenders for 30 minutes.
3. In a dish, mix the Parmesan cheese, pork rinds, paprika, Italian seasoning and garlic powder.
4. Preheat your air fryer to 390 degrees F.
5. Cover the chicken with the pork rind mixture.
6. Cook in the air fryer for 20 minutes, turning halfway through.

Serving Suggestion:

Serve with fresh green salad.

Tip:

You can also use bone-in chicken but increase cooking time to 5 to 10 minutes.

Nutritional Information Per Serving:

Calories: 378
Total fat: 20.7g
Saturated fat: 7.6g
Cholesterol: 121mg
Sodium: 563mg
Potassium: 262mg
Carbohydrates: 2.3g
Fiber: 0.2g
Protein: 47.4g
Sugars: 1g

Herbed Turkey

Serves: 14
Preparation and Cooking Time: 9 hours

Ingredients:

- 3/4 cup olive brine
- 1/2 cup buttermilk
- 3-1/2 lb. turkey breast fillets
- 2 sprigs fresh thyme

- 1 sprig fresh rosemary

Preparation:

1. Mix buttermilk and olive brine.
2. Soak the turkey in this mixture.
3. Add the herb sprigs. Refrigerate for 8 hours.
4. Preheat your air fryer to 350 degrees F.
5. Cook the turkey breast for 5 minutes.
6. Flip and cook for another 5 minutes.

Serving Suggestion:

Serve with cranberry sauce.

Nutritional Information Per Serving:

Calories: 141
Total Fat: 0.9g
Saturated Fat: 0.0g
Cholesterol: 82mg
Sodium: 62mg
Potassium: 326mg
Total Carbohydrates: 1.4g
Dietary Fiber: 0.6g
Protein: 30.2g
Sugars: 0g

Chapter 6: 15 Fish and Seafood Recipes

Nacho Shrimp

Serves: 6
Preparation and Cooking Time: 23 minutes

Ingredients:

- 1 egg, beaten
- 10 oz. corn chips, crushed
- 18 prawns, peeled and deveined

Preparation:

1. Add the egg to a bowl.
2. Place the corn chips in a dish.
3. Dip the prawns in egg and then dredge with the corn chips.
4. Preheat your air fryer to 350 degrees F.
5. Cook for 8 minutes.

Serving Suggestion:

Serve with guacamole and salsa.

Tip:

Check to see if the prawns are opaque. If not, extend cooking time.

Nutritional Information Per Serving:

Calories: 286
Total Fat: 14.5g
Saturated Fat: 3.0g
Cholesterol: 95mg
Sodium: 312mg
Potassium: 11mg
Total Carbohydrates: 28.9g
Dietary Fiber: 1.7g
Protein: 12.8g
Sugars: 2g

Fish Nuggets

Serves: 4
Preparation and Cooking Time: 35 minutes

Ingredients:

- Salt to taste
- 1/4 teaspoon ground dried chipotle pepper
- 1/4 cup maple syrup
- 1-1/2 cups garlic croutons
- 1 egg, beaten
- 1 lb. salmon fillet, sliced into small pieces
- Cooking spray

Preparation:

1. Mix the salt, chipotle pepper and maple syrup in a pan over low heat. Simmer for 10 minutes, stirring frequently.
2. Remove from heat and set aside.
3. Pulse croutons in a food processor until fully crushed.
4. Transfer to a dish.
5. Add the egg in another dish.
6. Preheat your air fryer to 390 degrees F.
7. Season the salmon with salt.
8. Dip in the salmon in the egg and then in

the croutons.
9. Spray with oil.
10. Cook in the air fryer for 3 minutes.
11. Shake and cook for another 4 minutes.

Serving Suggestion:

You can also serve chipotle maple syrup on the side.

Tip:

Use thick center-cut salmon fillets.

Nutritional Information Per Serving:

Calories: 364
Total Fat: 16.4g
Saturated Fat: 4.0g
Cholesterol: 115mg
Sodium: 353mg
Potassium: 509mg
Total Carbohydrates: 27.2g
Dietary Fiber: 0.8g
Protein: 25.8g
Sugars: 16g

Crispy Cod

Serves: 4
Preparation and Cooking Time: 25 minutes

Ingredients:

- 1 lb. cod, sliced into 4 pieces
- 1/4 cup polenta
- 1/4 cup all-purpose flour
- 1 teaspoon seafood seasoning
- 1-1/2 teaspoons garlic salt
- 1 teaspoon onion powder
- Pepper to taste
- 1/2 teaspoon paprika
- Cooking spray

Preparation:

1. Preheat your air fryer to 380 degrees F.
2. Dry the cod pieces with paper towel.
3. Mix the rest of the ingredients in a bowl.
4. Coat the cod pieces with the mixture.
5. Spray with oil.
6. Cook for 8 minutes.
7. Turn and cook for another 4 minutes.

Serving Suggestion:

Serve with coleslaw or roasted potatoes.

Nutritional Information Per Serving:

Calories: 171
Total Fat: 1.8g
Saturated Fat: 0.0g
Cholesterol: 42mg
Sodium: 1057mg
Potassium: 491mg
Total Carbohydrates: 14.8g
Dietary Fiber: 1.3g
Protein: 22.7g
Sugars: 1g

Lemon Garlic Lobster Tails

Serves: 2
Preparation and Cooking Time: 20 minutes

Ingredients:

- 8 oz. lobster tails
- 4 tablespoons butter
- 1 clove garlic, grated
- 1 teaspoon lemon zest

- Salt and pepper to taste
- 1 teaspoon parsley, chopped

Preparation:

1. Slice the lobster tails through the center and into the meat.
2. Spread the tails apart.
3. Add to the air fryer.
4. In a pan over medium heat, melt the butter and stir in the garlic and lemon zest.
5. Cook for 30 seconds.
6. Pour mixture over the lobster tails.
7. Season with salt and pepper.
8. Cook in the air fryer at 380 degrees F for 5 to 8 minutes.
9. Sprinkle with parsley.

Serving Suggestion:

Drizzle with lemon juice and garnish with lemon wedges.

Tip:

You can use frozen lobster tails.

Nutritional Information Per Serving:

Calories: 313
Total Fat: 25.8g
Saturated Fat: 16.0g
Cholesterol: 129mg
Sodium: 590mg
Potassium: 340mg
Total Carbohydrates: 3.3g
Dietary Fiber: 0.8g
Protein: 18.1g
Sugars: 0g

Sesame Cod

Serves: 4
Preparation and Cooking Time: 30 minutes

Ingredients:

- Vegetable oil
- 4 cod fillets
- Salt and pepper to taste
- 3 tablespoons butter, melted
- 2 tablespoons sesame seeds
- 3 cloves garlic, sliced thinly
- 12 oz. sugar snap peas

Preparation:

1. Grease the air fryer basket with oil.
2. Preheat air fryer to 400 degrees F.
3. Season with salt and pepper.
4. Mix the sesame seeds and butter in a bowl.
5. Take 2 tablespoons and set aside.
6. Toss the garlic and peas in the remaining mixture.
7. Add these to the air fryer.
8. Cook until tender.
9. Coat the fish with the reserved butter mixture.
10. Add to the air fryer.
11. Cook for 5 minutes.

Serving Suggestion:

Garnish with orange wedges.

Nutritional Information Per Serving:

Calories: 364

Total Fat: 15.2g
Saturated Fat: 6.0g
Cholesterol: 75mg
Sodium: 202mg
Potassium: 680mg

Total Carbohydrates: 22.9g
Dietary Fiber: 6.2g
Protein: 31.4g
Sugars: 4g

Fish Sticks

Serves: 4
Preparation and Cooking Time: 20 minutes

Ingredients:

- 1/4 cup all-purpose flour
- 1 egg, beaten
- 1/4 cup Parmesan cheese, grated
- 1/2 cup breadcrumbs
- 1 teaspoon paprika
- 1 tablespoon parsley
- Pepper to taste
- 1 lb. cod fillet, sliced into sticks
- Cooking spray

Preparation:

1. Preheat your Ninja air fryer to 400 degrees F.
2. Add the flour to a dish.
3. Place the egg in a bowl.
4. In another plate, mix the rest of the ingredients except the fish.
5. Dip the fish sticks in the flour, egg and then in the breadcrumb mixture.
6. Spray the air fryer basket with oil.
7. Cook the fish sticks for 5 minutes.
8. Flip and cook for another 5 minutes.

Serving Suggestion:

Serve with sweet chili or tartar sauce.

Tip:

You can also try using other types of white fish fillets.

Nutritional Information Per Serving:

Calories: 200
Total Fat: 4.1g
Saturated Fat: 1.0g
Cholesterol: 92mg
Sodium: 245mg
Potassium: 506mg
Total Carbohydrates: 16.5g
Dietary Fiber: 0.7g
Protein: 26.3g
Sugars: 0g

Coconut Shrimp

Serves: 6
Preparation and Cooking Time: 45 minutes

Ingredients:

- Pepper to taste
- 1/2 cup all-purpose flour
- 2 eggs, beaten
- 1/4 cup breadcrumbs
- 2/3 cup coconut flakes
- 12 oz. shrimp, peeled and deveined
- Cooking spray
- Salt to taste
- Chopped fresh cilantro

Preparation:

1. Mix the pepper and flour in a dish.
2. Add the eggs to a bowl.
3. In another plate, combine the breadcrumbs and coconut flakes.
4. Dip the shrimp in the first dish, second bowl and third plate.
5. Add to the air fryer basket.
6. Cook the shrimp in the air fryer at 400 degrees F for 3 minutes.
7. Flip and cook for another 3 minutes or until golden.
8. Season with salt and garnish with fresh cilantro.

Serving Suggestion:

Serve with honey lime dip.

Tip:

Keep the shrimp tails intact.

Nutritional Information Per Serving:

Calories: 236
Total Fat: 9.1g
Saturated Fat: 7.0g
Cholesterol: 147mg
Sodium: 316mg
Potassium: 200mg
Total Carbohydrates: 27.6g
Dietary Fiber: 2.2g
Protein: 13.8g
Sugars: 13g

Tuna Patties

Serves: 4
Preparation and Cooking Time: 25 minutes

Ingredients:

- Patties:
- 12 oz. tuna, minced
- 1 teaspoon onion, minced
- 1 teaspoon dried parsley
- Salt to taste
- 1 tablespoon green chives, chopped
- 1 tablespoon all-purpose flour
- Cooking spray

Preparation:

1. Combine all the ingredients in a bowl.
2. Form patties from this mixture.
3. Preheat your air fryer to 350 degrees F.
4. Spray the air fryer basket with oil.
5. Place in the air fryer and cook for 10 to 15 minutes.
6. Flip and cook for another 3 minutes.

Serving Suggestion:

Serve with cooked brown rice.

Tip:

You might need to increase cooking time if the patties are thick.

Nutritional Information Per Serving:

Calories: 351
Total Fat: 30.2g
Saturated Fat: 5.0g
Cholesterol: 52mg
Sodium: 568mg
Potassium: 317mg
Total Carbohydrates: 6.1g
Dietary Fiber: 1.4g

Protein: 15.6g   Sugars: 0g

Salmon Cakes with Spicy Mayo

Serves: 4
Preparation and Cooking Time: 40 minutes

Ingredients:

- Spicy mayo:
- 1/4 cup mayonnaise
- 1 tablespoon chili pepper sauce
- Salmon cakes:
- 1 lb. salmon fillets, flaked
- 1 egg, beaten
- 1/4 cup flour
- 1 green onion, chopped
- 1 teaspoon Old Bay seasoning
- Salt and pepper to taste
- Cooking spray

Preparation:

1. Blend the mayo and chili pepper sauce in a bowl.
2. Cover the bowl and refrigerate until ready to serve.
3. Mix all the salmon cake ingredients in another bowl.
4. Form patties from the mixture.
5. Cover the patties in wax paper.
6. Chill in the refrigerator for 15 minutes.
7. Preheat your air fryer to 390 degrees F.
8. Spray the air fryer basket with oil.
9. Add the patties to the basket and cook for 7 minutes.
10. Flip and cook for another 5 minutes.
11. Serve with the spicy mayo.

Serving Suggestion:

Garnish with chopped parsley.

Nutritional Information Per Serving:

Calories: 340
Total Fat: 24.7g
Saturated Fat: 4.0g
Cholesterol: 107mg
Sodium: 513mg
Potassium: 442mg
Total Carbohydrates: 3.6g
Dietary Fiber: 1.5g
Protein: 25.5g
Sugars: 1g

Fish Tacos

Serves: 4
Preparation and Cooking Time: 35 minutes

Ingredients:

- Cooking spray
- 4 cups cabbage slaw mix
- 1 tablespoon jalapeno pepper, chopped
- 1 tablespoon olive oil
- 1 tablespoon apple cider vinegar
- 1 tablespoon lime juice
- Salt and pepper to taste
- 1/4 cup all-purpose flour
- 1 lb. cod fillet, sliced into cubes

- 1/4 teaspoon ground cayenne pepper
- 2 tablespoons taco seasoning mix
- 1/4 cup cornmeal
- 8 corn tortillas

Preparation:

1. Preheat your air fryer to 400 degrees F.
2. Spray the air fryer basket with oil.
3. Toss the cabbage slaw mix and jalapeno pepper in olive oil, vinegar, lime juice, salt and pepper.
4. In another bowl, combine the rest of the ingredients.
5. Add the fish mixture in the air fryer basket.
6. Spray with oil.
7. Cook in the air fryer for 5 minutes.
8. Shake the basket.
9. Cook for another 5 minutes.
10. Transfer to a bowl. Set aside.
11. Add the cabbage mixture to the air fryer.
12. Cook for 8 minutes, shaking once.
13. Stuff corn tortillas with the fish mixture and cabbage slaw.

Serving Suggestion:

Garnish with chopped cilantro.

Tip:

You can also use whole-wheat tortillas and wrap the fish and cabbage slaw.

Nutritional Information Per Serving:

Calories: 370
Total Fat: 7.7g
Saturated Fat: 1.0g
Cholesterol: 47mg
Sodium: 740mg
Potassium: 717mg
Total Carbohydrates: 48.3g
Dietary Fiber: 5g
Protein: 25.7g
Sugars: 2g

Sweet Salmon

Serves: 2
Preparation and Cooking Time: 20 minutes

Ingredients:

- 2 salmon fillets
- Cooking spray
- 1 teaspoon brown sugar
- 1 tablespoon Cajun seasoning
- Salt to taste

Preparation:

1. Preheat your air fryer to 390 degrees F.
2. Spray your salmon fillets with oil.
3. Mix the brown sugar, seasoning and salt in a dish.
4. Season fish with this mixture.
5. Cook the fish in the air fryer for 8 minutes.
6. Flip and cook for another 2 minutes.

Serving Suggestion:

Let rest for 3 minutes before serving.

Nutritional Information Per Serving:

Calories: 327
Total Fat: 18.5g
Saturated Fat: 4.0g
Cholesterol: 99mg
Sodium: 811mg

Potassium: 655mg
Total Carbohydrates: 4g
Dietary Fiber: 0.3g

Protein: 33.7g
Sugars: 2g

Lemon Rosemary Fish

Serves: 4
Preparation and Cooking Time: 25 minutes

Ingredients:

- 1 cup dry bread crumbs
- 1/4 cup vegetable oil
- 4 fish fillets
- 1 egg, beaten
- 1 lemon, sliced
- 2 sprigs rosemary, chopped
- Salt to taste

Preparation:

1. Preheat your air fryer to 350 degrees F.
2. Combine the oil and breadcrumbs in a bowl.
3. Season the fish with salt.
4. Sprinkle with the chopped rosemary.
5. Dip in egg and coat with the breadcrumb mixture.
6. Cook in the air fryer for 6 minutes.
7. Flip and cook for another 6 minutes.

Serving Suggestion:

Add lemon slices on top before serving.

Tip:

Use salmon, tuna or any fish fillet for this recipe.

Nutritional Information Per Serving:

Calories: 354
Total Fat: 17.7g
Saturated Fat: 3.0g
Cholesterol: 107mg
Sodium: 309mg
Potassium: 415mg
Total Carbohydrates: 22.5g
Dietary Fiber: 2.5g
Protein: 26.9g

Pepper Shrimp

Serves: 4
Preparation and Cooking Time: 15 minutes

Ingredients:

- 1 tablespoon lemon juice
- 1 tablespoon olive oil
- 1/4 teaspoon garlic powder
- 1/4 teaspoon paprika
- 12 oz. shrimp, peeled and deveined

Preparation:

1. Preheat your air fryer to 400 degrees F.
2. Mix lemon juice, oil, garlic powder and paprika in a bowl.
3. Toss the shrimp in the mixture.
4. Cook in the air fryer for 8 minutes, shaking once.

Serving Suggestion:

Serve with pasta or salad, or as cold appetizer.

Nutritional Information Per Serving:

Calories: 215
Total Fat: 8.6g
Saturated Fat: 1.0g

Cholesterol: 255mg
Sodium: 528mg
Potassium: 414mg
Total Carbohydrates: 12.6g
Dietary Fiber: 5.5g
Protein: 28.9g
Sugars: 0g

Buttered Fish

Serves: 4
Preparation and Cooking Time: 20 minutes

Ingredients:

- 4 mahi mahi fillets
- Salt and pepper to taste
- Cooking spray
- 1/4 cup butter

Preparation:

1. Preheat your air fryer to 350 degrees F.
2. Sprinkle fish with salt and pepper.
3. Spray with oil.
4. Add to the basket.
5. Cook for 12 minutes.
6. While waiting, melt the butter in a pan over low heat.
7. Simmer for 3 minutes.

8. Drizzle the fish with butter before serving.

Serving Suggestion:

Garnish with rosemary sprigs.

Tip:

You can also use other white fish fillet.

Nutritional Information Per Serving:

Calories: 416
Total Fat: 31.9g
Saturated Fat: 20.0g
Cholesterol: 205mg
Sodium: 406mg
Potassium: 716mg
Total Carbohydrates: 0g
Dietary Fiber: 0g
Protein: 31.8g
Sugars: 0g

Fish with Pesto

Serves: 2
Preparation and Cooking Time: 20 minutes

Ingredients:

- 2 white fish fillets
- 1 tablespoon oil
- Salt and pepper to taste

- Pesto sauce:
- 2 cups basil leaves
- 2 cloves garlic
- 1 tablespoon walnuts
- 1 tablespoon Parmesan cheese, grated
- 1 cup olive oil

Preparation:

1. Preheat your air fryer to 350 degrees F.
2. Coat the fish with oil.
3. Sprinkle with salt and pepper.
4. Add to the air fryer basket.
5. Cook for 8 minutes.
6. Add the basil leaves to the food processor along with the rest of the ingredients.
7. Pulse until smooth.
8. Spread pesto on top of the fish.

Serving Suggestion:

You can also serve the pesto on the side.

Nutritional Information Per Serving:

Calories: 1302
Total Fat: 123.5g
Saturated Fat: 18.0g
Cholesterol: 58mg
Sodium: 1773mg
Potassium: 890mg
Total Carbohydrates: 3.1g
Dietary Fiber: 1.1g
Protein: 43.3g
Sugars: 0g

Chapter 7: 15 Vegan and Vegetarian Recipes

Roasted Veggies

Serves: 4
Preparation and Cooking Time: 30 minutes

Ingredients:

- 1 onion, sliced into wedges
- 4 mushrooms, sliced in half
- 1 red bell pepper, sliced
- 1 zucchini, sliced
- 1 summer squash, sliced
- 1 tablespoon olive oil
- Salt and pepper to taste

Preparation:

1. Preheat your air fryer to 370 degrees F.
2. Add all the vegetables in a bowl.
3. Drizzle with olive oil and season with salt and pepper.
4. Cook in the air fryer for 10 minutes.
5. Shake and cook for another 10 minutes.

Serving Suggestion:

Serve as side dish or turn it into a salad.

Nutritional Information Per Serving:

Calories: 69
Total Fat: 3.8g
Saturated Fat: 1.0g
Cholesterol: 0mg
Sodium: 48mg
Potassium: 436mg
Total Carbohydrates: 7.7g
Dietary Fiber: 2.3g
Protein: 2.6g
Sugars: 4g

Zucchini Chips

Serves: 4
Preparation and Cooking Time: 35 minutes

Ingredients:

- 3/4 cup Parmesan cheese, grated
- 1 cup panko bread crumbs
- 1 zucchini, sliced thinly
- 1 egg, beaten
- Cooking spray

Preparation:

1. Preheat your air fryer to 350 degrees F.
2. Mix the Parmesan cheese and breadcrumbs on a dish.
3. Dip the zucchini in the egg and then dredge with the cheese mixture.
4. Spray the chips with oil.
5. Add to the air fryer.
6. Cook for 10 minutes.
7. Flip and cook for another 2 minutes.

Serving Suggestion:

Serve with marinara sauce.

Tip:

Turn this recipe into vegan by using egg product in place of egg and vegan cheese instead of Parmesan.

Nutritional Information Per Serving:

Calories: 159

Total Fat: 6.6g
Saturated Fat: 3.0g
Cholesterol: 60mg
Sodium: 384mg
Potassium: 164mg
Total Carbohydrates: 21.1g
Dietary Fiber: 0.5g
Protein: 10.8g
Sugars: 1g

Seasoned Potato Wedges

Serves: 4
Preparation and Cooking Time: 35 minutes

Ingredients:

- 2 potatoes, sliced into wedges
- 1-1/2 tablespoons olive oil
- Salt and pepper to taste
- 1/2 teaspoon parsley
- 1/2 teaspoon paprika
- 1/2 teaspoon chilli powder

Preparation:

1. Preheat your air fryer to 400 degrees F. Toss the potatoes in oil.
2. Season with salt and pepper.
3. Sprinkle with parsley, paprika and chilli powder.
4. Add to the air fryer basket.
5. Cook for 10 minutes.
6. Flip and cook for another 5 minutes.

Serving Suggestion:

Serve with vegan friendly dip.

Tip:

Slice potatoes first in half, and then slice again to create wedges.

Nutritional Information Per Serving:

Calories: 129
Total Fat: 5.3g
Saturated Fat: 1.0g
Cholesterol: 0mg
Sodium: 230mg
Potassium: 466mg
Total Carbohydrates: 19g
Dietary Fiber: 2.6g
Protein: 2.3g
Sugars: 1g

Baked Potatoes

Serves: 2
Preparation and Cooking Time: 1 hour and 5 minutes

Ingredients:

- 2 potatoes
- 1 tablespoon peanut oil
- Salt to taste

Preparation:

1. Preheat your air fryer to 400 degrees F. Brush with oil and season with salt.
2. Add these to the air fryer basket.
3. Cook for 1 hour.

Serving Suggestion:

Serve with sour cream (for vegetarians) or vegan friendly dips.

Tip:

Do not prick the potatoes before or during cooking.

Nutritional Information Per Serving:

Calories: 344
Total Fat: 7.1g
Saturated Fat: 1.0g
Cholesterol: 0mg
Sodium: 462mg
Potassium: 1557mg
Total Carbohydrates: 64.5g
Dietary Fiber: 8.1g
Protein: 7.5g
Sugars: 3g

Roasted Cauliflower

Serves: 2
Preparation and Cooking Time: 25 minutes

Ingredients:

- 1 tablespoon peanut oil
- 3 cloves garlic, crushed
- 1/2 teaspoon paprika
- Salt to taste
- 4 cups cauliflower florets

Preparation:

1. Preheat your air fryer to 400 degrees F.
2. Mix the oil, garlic, paprika and salt in a bowl.
3. Coat the cauliflower florets in this mixture.
4. Add to the air fryer.
5. Cook for 15 minutes, shaking once or twice.

Serving Suggestion:

Serve as side dish to a main course.

Tip:

Test the cauliflower for crunchiness. If you want it crunchier, add 5 more minutes of cooking time.

Nutritional Information Per Serving:

Calories: 118
Total Fat: 7g
Saturated Fat: 1.0g
Cholesterol: 0mg
Sodium: 642mg
Potassium: 638mg
Total Carbohydrates: 12.4g
Dietary Fiber: 5.3g
Protein: 4.3g
Sugars: 5g

Spicy Green Beans

Serves: 4
Preparation and Cooking Time: 40 minutes

Ingredients:

- 12 oz. green beans, trimmed
- 1 teaspoon soy sauce
- 1 tablespoon sesame oil
- 1 clove garlic, crushed and minced
- 1 teaspoon rice wine vinegar
- 1/2 teaspoon crushed red pepper

Preparation:

1. Preheat your air fryer to 400 degrees F.
2. Add green beans in a bowl.
3. Mix the rest of the ingredients and pour into the green beans.
4. Coat evenly.
5. Marinate for 5 minutes.
6. Add green beans to the air fryer basket.
7. Cook for 12 minutes, shaking once or twice.

Serving Suggestion:

Serve while warm or reheat before serving.

Tip:

Cook in batches to ensure even cooking.

Nutritional Information Per Serving:

Calories: 59
Total Fat: 3.6g
Saturated Fat: 1.0g
Cholesterol: 0mg
Sodium: 80mg
Potassium: 192mg
Total Carbohydrates: 6.6g
Dietary Fiber: 3g
Protein: 1.7g
Sugars: 1g

French Fries

Serves: 4
Preparation and Cooking Time: 40 minutes

Ingredients:

6 potatoes, sliced into fries
1 tablespoon olive oil
Salt to taste

Preparation:

Preheat your air fryer to 320 degrees F.
Toss the potatoes in oil.
Cook in the air fryer basket for 20 minutes.
Shake and cook for another 10 minutes.
Season with salt before serving.

Serving Suggestion:

Serve with ketchup and mustard, or if vegan, vegan friendly dip.

Tip:

Soak the potato sticks in water before cooking.

Nutritional Information Per Serving:

Calories: 184
Total Fat: 3.6g
Saturated Fat: 1.0g
Cholesterol: 0mg
Sodium: 51mg
Potassium: 842mg
Total Carbohydrates: 34.9g
Dietary Fiber: 4.4g
Protein: 4g
Sugars: 2g

Roasted Brussels Sprouts

Serves: 2
Preparation and Cooking Time: 20 minutes

Ingredients:

- Salt and pepper to taste
- 1 teaspoon avocado oil
- 10 oz. Brussels sprouts, sliced in half
- 1 teaspoon balsamic vinegar

Preparation:

1. Preheat your air fryer to 350 degrees F.
2. Mix salt, pepper and oil.
3. Toss the Brussels sprouts in this mixture.
4. Cook in the air fryer for 5 minutes.
5. Shake and cook for another 5 minutes.
6. Drizzle with balsamic vinegar before serving.

Serving Suggestion:

Serve as a side dish or as main course.

Tip:

If you want softer veggies, add 5 more minutes to cooking time.

Nutritional Information Per Serving:

Calories: 94
Total Fat: 3.4g
Saturated Fat: 1.0g
Cholesterol: 2mg
Sodium: 691mg
Potassium: 553mg
Total Carbohydrates: 13.3g
Dietary Fiber: 5.5g
Protein: 5.8g
Sugars: 3g

Sweet Potato Fries

Serves: 2
Preparation and Cooking Time: 20 minutes

Ingredients:

- 2 sweet potatoes, sliced into fries
- 1 tablespoon vegetable oil
- Pinch sweet paprika
- Pinch garlic powder
- Salt and pepper to taste

Preparation:

1. Preheat your air fryer to 400 degrees F.
2. Toss the sweet potatoes in oil.
3. Season with the paprika, garlic powder, salt and pepper.
4. Cook in the air fryer for 10 minutes or until golden, shaking once or twice.

Serving Suggestion:

Serve with ketchup or with vegan-friendly dip.

Tip:

Soak sweet potatoes in water for 10 minutes before cooking.

Nutritional Information Per Serving:

Calories: 119
Total Fat: 7.1g
Saturated Fat: 1.0g
Cholesterol: 0mg
Sodium: 516mg
Potassium: 228mg
Total Carbohydrates: 13.5g
Dietary Fiber: 2.1g
Protein: 1.1g
Sugars: 3g

Roasted Okra

Serves: 1
Preparation and Cooking Time: 20 minutes

Ingredients:

- 1/2 lb. okra, trimmed and pods removed
- 1 teaspoon olive oil
- Salt and pepper to taste

Preparation:

1. Preheat your air fryer to 350 degrees F.
2. Toss the okra in oil and season with salt and pepper.
3. Add to the air fryer basket.
4. Cook for 7 minutes.
5. Toss and cook for another 5 minutes.

Serving Suggestion:

Serve with mixture of soy sauce and vinegar.

Tip:

Add 2 more minutes of cooking time if you want okra softer.

Nutritional Information Per Serving:

Calories: 113
Total Fat: 5g

Saturated Fat: 1.0g
Cholesterol: 0mg
Sodium: 600mg
Potassium: 691mg

Total Carbohydrates: 16.1g
Dietary Fiber: 7.3g
Protein: 4.6g
Sugars: 3g

Avocado Fries

Serves: 2
Preparation and Cooking Time: 20 minutes

Ingredients:

- 1/4 cup all-purpose flour
- Salt and pepper to taste
- 1 egg
- 1 teaspoon water
- 1 avocado, sliced into fries
- 1/2 cup panko breadcrumbs
- Cooking spray

Calories: 319
Total Fat: 18g
Saturated Fat: 3.0g
Cholesterol: 82mg
Sodium: 463mg
Potassium: 540mg
Total Carbohydrates: 39.8g
Dietary Fiber: 7.3g
Protein: 9.3g
Sugars: 1g

Preparation:

1. Preheat your air fryer to 400 degrees F.
2. Combine salt, pepper and flour in a bowl.
3. In another bowl, beat the egg and water.
4. Add the breadcrumbs to another bowl.
5. Coat the avocado fries with the flour mixture, then dip in the egg mixture.
6. Finally, dredge with the breadcrumbs.
7. Spray the fries with oil before placing in the air fryer basket.
8. Cook for 4 minutes.
9. Turn and cook for another 3 minutes.

Serving Suggestion:

Serve with garlic aioli.

Tip:

Replace egg with egg product to make recipe vegan friendly.

Nutritional Information Per Serving:

Eggplant Parmesan

Serves: 4
Preparation and Cooking Time: 35 minutes

Ingredients:

- 1/2 cup breadcrumbs
- 1/2 teaspoon onion powder
- 1/2 teaspoon garlic powder
- 1/2 teaspoon dried basil
- 1 teaspoon Italian seasoning
- Salt and pepper to taste
- 1/4 cup Parmesan cheese, grated
- 1/4 cup flour
- 2 eggs, beaten
- 1 eggplant, sliced into rounds
- 1 cup marinara sauce

Preparation:

1. Mix the breadcrumbs, onion powder, garlic powder, basil, Italian seasoning, salt and pepper in a bowl.
2. Add flour to a dish.
3. Add the eggs to another bowl.
4. Dip eggplant slices in the flour, eggs and bredcrumbs.
5. Preheat your air fryer to 370 degrees F.
6. Add these to the air fryer basket.
7. Cook for 10 minutes.
8. Flip and cook for another 5 minutes.
9. Spread eggplant slices with marinara sauce and cheese.
10. Put these back to the air fryer basket.
11. Cook until the cheese has melted.

Serving Suggestion:

Serve with leafy green salad.

Tip:

Remove cheese or use vegan cheese, and replace egg with egg product to turn this vegetarian recipe into vegan.

Nutritional Information Per Serving:

Calories: 377
Total Fat: 15.7g
Saturated Fat: 8.0g
Cholesterol: 135mg
Sodium: 1563mg
Potassium: 662mg
Total Carbohydrates: 35.5g
Dietary Fiber: 7.5g
Protein: 24.3g
Sugars: 11g

Roasted Asparagus & Mushrooms

Serves: 4
Preparation and Cooking Time: 35 minutes

Ingredients:

- 1/2 cup red bell pepper, diced
- 1/2 cup mushrooms, diced
- 1/2 cup cauliflower, diced
- 1/2 cup summer squash, diced
- 1/2 cup zucchini, diced
- 1/2 cup asparagus, diced
- 2 teaspoons vegetable oil
- 1/4 teaspoon Italian seasoning
- Salt and pepper to taste

Preparation:

1. Preheat your air fryer to 360 degrees F.

2. Stir veggies in oil and seasonings.
3. Transfer in the air fryer basket.
4. Cook for 10 minutes.
5. Stir and cook for another 5 minutes.

Nutritional Information Per Serving:

Calories: 37
Total Fat: 2.4g
Saturated Fat: 0.0g
Cholesterol: 0mg
Sodium: 152mg
Potassium: 203mg
Total Carbohydrates: 3.4g
Dietary Fiber: 1.3g
Protein: 1.4g
Sugars: 2g

Zucchini Gratin

Serves: 4
Preparation and Cooking Time: 25 minutes

Ingredients:

- 2 zucchini, sliced
- 2 tablespoons breadcrumbs
- 1 tablespoon parsley, chopped
- 1 tablespoon vegetable oil
- 4 tablespoons Parmesan cheese, grated
- Salt and pepper to taste

Preparation:

1. Preheat your air fryer to 360 degrees F.
2. Arrange the zucchini in the air fryer basket.
3. Mix the rest of the ingredients in a bowl.
4. Spread mixture on top of the zucchini.
5. Cook for 15 minutes or until golden.

Serving Suggestion:

Sprinkle with chopped parsley.

Nutritional Information Per Serving:

Calories: 82
Total Fat: 5.2g
Saturated Fat: 1.0g
Cholesterol: 4mg
Sodium: 111mg
Potassium: 278mg
Total Carbohydrates: 6.1g
Dietary Fiber: 1.3g
Protein: 3.6g
Sugars: 2g

Eggplant Fries

Serves: 4
Preparation and Cooking Time: 35 minutes

Ingredients:

- 1/2 cup Italian bread crumbs
- 1 teaspoon Italian seasoning
- 1/2 teaspoon dried basil
- 1/2 teaspoon onion powder
- 1/2 teaspoon garlic powder
- 1/4 cup Parmesan cheese, grated
- Salt and pepper to taste
- 1/4 cup all-purpose flour
- 2 eggs, beaten
- 1 eggplant, sliced into thick fries

Preparation:

1. In a bowl, mix the breadcrumbs, Italian seasoning, basil, onion powder, garlic powder, cheese, salt and pepper.
2. Add flour to the second dish and the eggs in a bowl.
3. Dip the eggplant fries in the flour, then in the eggs and finally, coat with the breadcrumb mixture.
4. Preheat your air fryer to 370 degrees F.
5. Add the eggplant fries to the basket.
6. Cook for 10 minutes.
7. Shake and cook for another 5 minutes.

Serving Suggestion:

Serve with ketchup or marinara sauce.

Tip:

Replace cheese with vegan cheese if you are a vegan.

Nutritional Information Per Serving:

Calories: 180
Total Fat: 5.1g
Saturated Fat: 2.0g
Cholesterol: 98mg
Sodium: 960mg
Potassium: 418mg
Total Carbohydrates: 25.4g
Dietary Fiber: 5.9g
Protein: 9.6g
Sugars: 5g

Chapter 8: 20 Appetizers

Asparagus Fries

Serves: 6
Preparation and Cooking Time: 20 minutes

Ingredients:

- 1 teaspoon honey
- 1 egg, beaten
- 1/2 cup Parmesan cheese, grated
- 1 cup panko bread crumbs
- 12 asparagus, trimmed and sliced in 2
- 1/4 cup Greek yogurt
- 1/4 cup mustard

Preparation:

1. Preheat your air fryer to 400 degrees F.
2. Mix honey and egg in a bowl.
3. In another bowl, combine the cheese and breadcrumbs.
4. Dip the asparagus in the egg mixture, and then cover with the breadcrumb mixture.
5. Add these to the air fryer and cook for 5 minutes.
6. Mix the yogurt and mustard.
7. Serve asparagus fries with dip.

Serving Suggestion:

Garnish with leafy greens.

Tip:

Shake the air fryer basket to ensure even cooking.

Nutritional Information Per Serving:

Calories: 120
Total Fat: 4.3g
Saturated Fat: 2.0g
Cholesterol: 39mg
Sodium: 365mg
Potassium: 110mg
Total Carbohydrates: 18g
Dietary Fiber: 2.1g
Protein: 7.5g
Sugars: 3g

Yam Fries with Spicy Sour Cream Sauce

Serves: 4
Preparation and Cooking Time: 36 minutes

Ingredients:

- 1-1/4 lb. purple yam, sliced into fries
- 2 teaspoons olive oil
- Salt to taste
- 1/4 cup sour cream
- 2 teaspoons chili pepper sauce

Preparation:

1. Preheat your air fryer to 320 degrees F.
2. Toss the yam in oil and salt.
3. Add to the air fryer basket.
4. Cook for 16 minutes.
5. Increase temperature to 400 degrees.
6. Cook for another 5 minutes.
7. Combine sour cream and chili pepper sauce.
8. Serve fries with dip.

Tip:

Use French fry cutter for convenience.

Nutritional Information Per Serving:

Calories: 242
Total Fat: 6.7g
Saturated Fat: 3.0g
Cholesterol: 8mg
Sodium: 719mg
Potassium: 1263mg
Total Carbohydrates: 43.3g
Dietary Fiber: 6.3g
Protein: 2.9g
Sugars: 1g

Tempura Vegetables

Serves: 4
Preparation and Cooking Time: 35 minutes

Ingredients:

- 1/2 cup all-purpose flour
- Salt and pepper to taste
- 2 tablespoons water
- 2 eggs, beaten
- 1 cup panko bread crumbs
- 2 teaspoons vegetable oil
- 1 cup green beans
- 1 cup asparagus spears
- 1 cup white onion rings

Preparation:

1. Combine the salt, pepper and flour in a dish.
2. In another bowl, mix water and eggs.
3. Combine the oil and breadcrumbs in another dish.
4. Dip the veggies in the flour mixture, egg mixture and then in the breadcrumb mixture.
5. Preheat your air fryer to 400 degrees F.
6. Cook veggies until golden brown.

Serving Suggestion:

Serve with your favorite dip.

Tip:

Sprinkle with a little salt before serving.

Nutritional Information Per Serving:

Calories: 247
Total Fat: 10.1g
Saturated Fat: 2.0g
Cholesterol: 93mg
Sodium: 464mg
Potassium: 339mg
Total Carbohydrates: 37.7g
Dietary Fiber: 3.9g
Protein: 9.3g
Sugars: 2g

Cheesy Stuffed Mushrooms

Serves: 24
Preparation and Cooking Time: 45 minutes

Ingredients:

- 24 mushrooms, stems removed and set aside
- 1/2 onion, diced

- 1 red bell pepper, diced
- 2 slices bacon, chopped
- 1 carrot, diced
- 1/2 cup sour cream
- 1 cup Cheddar, grated

Preparation:

1. Chop the mushroom stems and combine with the onion, red bell pepper, bacon and carrot.
2. Transfer to a pan over medium heat.
3. Cook for 5 minutes.
4. Stir in the sour cream and cheddar.
5. Cook for 2 minutes.
6. Preheat your air fryer to 350 degrees F.
7. Stuff the mushrooms with the mixture.
8. Arrange the mushrooms in the air fryer basket.
9. Cook for 8 minutes.

Tip:

You can also use mozzarella in place of cheddar but use this to top the mushrooms.

Nutritional Information Per Serving:

Calories: 43
Total Fat: 3.1g
Saturated Fat: 2.0g
Cholesterol: 8mg
Sodium: 55mg
Potassium: 92mg
Total Carbohydrates: 1.7g
Dietary Fiber: 0.3g
Protein: 2.4g
Sugars: 1g

Mozzarella Bites

Serves: 6
Preparation and Cooking Time: 1 hour and 20 minutes

Ingredients:

- 1 tablespoon water
- 1 egg, beaten
- 1/2 cup all-purpose flour
- 1/2 teaspoon dried Italian seasoning
- 1/2 teaspoon salt
- 3/4 cup panko bread crumbs
- 6 mozzarella slices
- Cooking spray

Preparation:

1. Mix water and egg in a bowl.
2. In a plate, combine flour, Italian seasoning and salt.
3. Add the breadcrumbs in another plate.
4. Dip the mozzarella slices in the egg mixture.
5. Coat with the flour mixture.
6. Dip once again in the egg mixture, then dredge with breadcrumbs.
7. Preheat your air fryer to 360 degrees F.
8. Coat cheese slices with oil.
9. Cook in the air fryer basket for 5 minutes.

Serving Suggestion:

Serve with marinara sauce.

Tip:

You can make this recipe ahead of time and freeze for up to 1 month.

Nutritional Information Per Serving:

Calories: 183

Total Fat: 6.7g
Saturated Fat: 3.0g
Cholesterol: 46mg
Sodium: 574mg
Potassium: 147mg

Total Carbohydrates: 22.6g
Dietary Fiber: 1.2g
Protein: 10.9g
Sugars: 3g

Stuffed Peppers

Serves: 20
Preparation and Cooking Time: 1 hour and 5 minutes

Ingredients:

- 2 tablespoons olive oil, divided
- 8 oz. Italian sausage
- 16 oz. large sweet peppers, tops sliced off
- 1 garlic, crushed and minced
- 1/2 cup cheddar cheese, shredded
- 8 oz. cream cheese
- 2 tablespoons breadcrumbs
- 1 tablespoon chives, chopped
- Pepper to taste

Preparation:

1. Pour half of oil in a pan over medium heat.
2. Cook the sausage for 5 minutes.
3. Drain and set aside.
4. Brush sweet peppers with remaining oil.
5. Add to the air fryer basket.
6. Cook at 350 degrees F for 3 minutes.
7. Let cool.
8. In a bowl, mix the sausage with the rest of the ingredients.
9. Stuff the peppers with the mixture.
10. Cook in the air fryer for 3 minutes.

Serving Suggestion:

Let cool before serving.

Nutritional Information Per Serving:

Calories: 101
Total Fat: 8.6g
Saturated Fat: 4.0g
Cholesterol: 20mg
Sodium: 159mg
Potassium: 43mg
Total Carbohydrates: 2.6g
Dietary Fiber: 0.3g
Protein: 3.6g
Sugars: 0g

Cauliflower Tots

Serves: 4
Preparation and Cooking Time: 25 minutes

Ingredients:

- Cooking spray
- 16 oz. cauliflower tots

Preparation:

1. Preheat your air fryer to 400 degrees F.
2. Spray the air fryer basket with oil.
3. Add cauliflower tots in the air fryer basket.
4. Cook for 6 minutes.
5. Flip and cook for another 3 minutes.

Serving Suggestion:

Serve with ketchup.

Nutritional Information Per Serving:

Calories: 147
Total Fat: 6.1g
Saturated Fat: 1.0g

Cholesterol: 0mg
Sodium: 494mg
Total Carbohydrates: 20g
Dietary Fiber: 6.7g
Protein: 2.7g
Sugars: 0g

Beer Battered Green Beans with Spicy Sauce

Serves: 4
Preparation and Cooking Time: 30 minutes

Ingredients:

- Salt and pepper to taste
- 1 cup all-purpose flour
- 1 cup beer
- 12 oz. green beans
- Sauce:
- 1 teaspoon horseradish
- 2 teaspoons hot sauce
- 1 cup ranch dressing

Preparation:

1. Combine the salt, pepper, flour and beer in a bowl.
2. Cover the beans with this mixture.
3. Preheat your air fryer to 400 degrees F.
4. Cook for 10 minutes, shaking once or twice.
5. Mix the sauce ingredients and serve with the green beans.

Serving Suggestion:

You can also serve with other dips like mayo mustard or marinara sauce.

Tip:

Cook in batches to ensure even cooking.

Nutritional Information Per Serving:

Calories: 466
Total Fat: 31.6g
Saturated Fat: 5.0g
Cholesterol: 16mg
Sodium: 1863mg
Potassium: 263mg
Total Carbohydrates: 35.4g
Dietary Fiber: 4.1g
Protein: 5.9g
Sugars: 4g

Fried Tomatoes

Serves: 4
Preparation and Cooking Time: 20 minutes

Ingredients:

- Cooking spray
- 1 egg, beaten
- 1/4 cup flour
- 1/2 cup cornmeal
- Salt and pepper to taste
- 1/4 cup panko breadcrumbs
- 2 green tomatoes, sliced

Preparation:

1. Preheat your air fryer to 400 degrees F.
2. Spray air fryer basket with oil.
3. Add egg in a dish.
4. In another dish, mix the flour, cornmeal, salt, pepper and breadcrumbs.
5. Dip the tomato slice in the egg and then with the cornmeal mixture.
6. Spray with oil.
7. Cook for 8 minutes.
8. Flip and cook for another 4 minutes.

Serving Suggestion:

Drain in paper towel lined plate before serving.

Nutritional Information Per Serving:

Calories: 144
Total Fat: 2.2g
Saturated Fat: 1.0g
Cholesterol: 46mg
Sodium: 777mg
Potassium: 189mg
Total Carbohydrates: 28.7g
Dietary Fiber: 2g
Protein: 5.5g
Sugars: 3g

Garlic Mushrooms

Serves: 2
Preparation and Cooking Time: 20 minutes

Ingredients:

- 8 oz. cremini mushrooms, sliced in half
- 2 tablespoons avocado oil
- 1 teaspoon soy sauce
- 1/2 teaspoon garlic granules
- Salt and pepper to taste

Preparation:

1. Preheat your air fryer to 200 degrees F.
2. Mix all the ingredients in a bowl.
3. Transfer to the air fryer basket.
4. Cook for 10 minutes, shaking once or twice.

Serving Suggestion:

Sprinkle chopped parsley on top.

Tip:

Choose mushrooms of the same size.

Nutritional Information Per Serving:

Calories: 152
Total Fat: 14.4g
Saturated Fat: 2.0g
Cholesterol: 0mg
Sodium: 172mg
Potassium: 371mg
Total Carbohydrates: 4.5g
Dietary Fiber: 1.3g
Protein: 3.7g
Sugars: 2g

Spiralized Potatoes

Serves: 4

Preparation and Cooking Time: 1 hour

Ingredients:

- 2 potatoes
- 1 tablespoon vegetable oil
- Salt and pepper to taste

Preparation:

1. Slice potatoes using spiralizer.
2. Toss potatoes in oil, salt and pepper.
3. Preheat your air fryer to 360 degrees F.
4. Cook in the air fryer for 5 minutes.
5. Increase temperature to 380 degrees F.
6. Flip spirals and cook for another 10 minutes.

Serving Suggestion:

Serve with mayo or ketchup.

Tip:

Soak potatoes for 20 minutes before cooking.

Nutritional Information Per Serving:

Calories: 113
Total Fat: 3.6g
Saturated Fat: 0g
Cholesterol: 0mg
Sodium: 106mg
Total Carbohydrates: 18.6g
Dietary Fiber: 2g
Protein: 2.2g
Potassium: 530mg
Sugars: 1g

Onion Rings

Serves: 4
Preparation and Cooking Time: 25 minutes

Ingredients:

- 1 teaspoon salt
- 1/2 cup cornstarch
- 2 teaspoons baking powder
- 3/4 cup all-purpose flour
- 4 cups white onion rings
- 1 egg, beaten
- 1 cup milk
- 1 cup breadcrumbs
- Cooking spray
- Pinch garlic powder

Preparation:

1. Mix the salt, cornstarch, baking powder and flour in a plate.
2. Coat the onion rings with this mixture.
3. In another bowl, mix the eggs and milk.
4. Dip the onion rings in this mixture.
5. Coat with breadcrumbs.
6. Spray with oil.
7. Cook in the air fryer at 400 degrees F for 3 minutes.
8. Flip and cook for another 2 minutes.
9. Season with garlic powder before serving.

Serving Suggestion:

Serve with tartar sauce.

Tip:

You can make this ahead and freeze breaded onions rings for up to 1 month.

Nutritional Information Per Serving:

Calories: 321
Total Fat: 4.3g

Saturated Fat: 2.0g

Cholesterol: 51mg

Sodium: 1069mg

Potassium: 259mg

Total Carbohydrates: 59.7g

Dietary Fiber: 2.9g

Protein: 10.2g

Sugars: 6g

Fried Pickles

Serves: 8

Preparation and Cooking Time: 20 minutes

Ingredients:

- Sauce:
- 1/2 cup mayonnaise
- 2 tablespoons hot sauce
- Pickles:
- 16 oz. dill pickle chips
- 1 egg
- 2 tablespoons milk
- 1/2 cup cornmeal
- 1/2 cup all-purpose flour
- 1/4 teaspoon garlic powder
- 1/4 teaspoon paprika
- Salt and pepper to taste
- Cooking spray

Preparation:

1. Combine mayo and hot sauce in a bowl.
2. Cover and refrigerate.
3. Preheat your air fryer to 400 degrees F.
4. Drain the pickles. Dry using paper towels.
5. Combine milk and egg in a bowl.
6. Mix cornmeal, flour, garlic powder, paprika, salt and pepper.
7. Dip the pickles in the egg mixture and then in the cornmeal mixture.
8. Spray with oil.
9. Cook in the air fryer for 4 minutes.
10. Flip and cook for another 4 minutes.
11. Serve with reserved sauce.

Serving Suggestion:

Garnish with lemon wedges.

Tip:

You can skip the hot sauce if you don't like it spicy.

Nutritional Information Per Serving:

Calories: 178

Total Fat: 12g

Saturated Fat: 2.0g

Cholesterol: 26mg

Sodium: 1024mg

Potassium: 114mg

Total Carbohydrates: 15.4g

Dietary Fiber: 1.6g

Protein: 2.7g

Sugars: 1g

Crispy Mozzarella Sticks

Serves: 6

Preparation and Cooking Time: 1 hour and 30 minutes

Ingredients:

- Batter:

- 1 tablespoon cornmeal
- 5 tablespoons cornstarch
- 1/4 cup all-purpose flour
- 1/2 cup water
- Salt to taste
- 1 teaspoon garlic powder
- Coating:
- 1 cup panko bread crumbs
- 1/2 teaspoon parsley flakes
- 1/4 teaspoon onion powder
- 1/2 teaspoon garlic powder
- 1/4 teaspoon dried basil
- 1/4 teaspoon dried oregano
- Salt and pepper to taste
- Cheese:
- 5 oz. mozzarella cheese sliced into sticks
- 1 tablespoon all-purpose flour
- Cooking spray

Preparation:

1. Combine the batter ingredients in a bowl.
2. Mix the coating ingredients in another bowl.
3. Dip the cheese sticks in flour.
4. Toss in the batter mixture, and then finally in the coating mixture.
5. Freeze for 1 hour.
6. Preheat your air fryer to 400 degrees F.
7. Spray cheese with oil.
8. Cook for 6 minutes.
9. Flip and cook for another 7 minutes.

Serving Suggestion:

Season with garlic salt before serving.

Tip:

You can also use vegan mozzarella.

Nutritional Information Per Serving:

Calories: 246
Total Fat: 6.8g
Saturated Fat: 4.0g
Cholesterol: 23mg
Sodium: 936mg
Potassium: 66mg
Total Carbohydrates: 39.2g
Dietary Fiber: 0.7g
Protein: 12.9g
Sugars: 1g

Spicy Pickle Fries

Serves: 12
Preparation and Cooking Time: 30 minutes

Ingredients:

- 16 oz. dill pickle spears
- 1/2 teaspoon paprika
- 1 cup all-purpose flour
- 1/4 cup milk
- 1 egg, beaten
- 1 cup panko bread crumbs
- Cooking spray

Preparation:

1. Dry pickles with paper towel.
2. Mix the paprika and flour in a bowl.
3. Combine egg and milk in another bowl.
4. Add the breadcrumbs to a plate.
5. Preheat your air fryer to 400 degrees F.
6. Dip the pickles in the flour mixture, egg mixture and coat with the breadcrumbs.

7. Spray these with oil.
8. Cook in the air fryer for 14 minutes.
9. Flip and cook for another 3 minutes.

Serving Suggestion:

Serve with ranch dressing.

Nutritional Information Per Serving:

Calories: 80
Total Fat: 1g
Saturated Fat: 0.0g
Cholesterol: 16mg
Sodium: 770mg
Potassium: 92mg
Total Carbohydrates: 16.8g
Dietary Fiber: 1g
Protein: 3.1g
Sugars: 1g

Herbed Potato Sticks

Serves: 4
Preparation and Cooking Time: 30 minutes

Ingredients:

- 2 potatoes, sliced into strips
- 1 tablespoon oil
- 1/2 tablespoon dried rosemary
- 1/2 tablespoon dried oregano
- 1/2 tablespoon dried basil
- Salt to taste

Preparation:

1. Preheat your air fryer to 380 degrees F.
2. Toss the potatoes in oil.
3. Sprinkle with the rest of the ingredients.
4. Add to the air fryer basket.
5. Cook for 10 minutes.
6. Flip and cook for another 5 minutes or until golden.

Serving Suggestion:

Serve with mayo mustard dip.

Nutritional Information Per Serving:

Calories: 115
Total Fat: 3.5g
Saturated Fat: 1.0g
Cholesterol: 0mg
Sodium: 465mg
Potassium: 461mg
Total Carbohydrates: 19.2g
Dietary Fiber: 2.5g
Protein: 2.2g
Sugars: 1g

Asian Deviled Eggs

Serves: 2
Preparation and Cooking Time: 40 minutes

Ingredients:

6 eggs
1-1/2 teaspoons sesame oil
1-1/2 teaspoons sriracha sauce
2 tablespoons mayonnaise
1 teaspoon Dijon mustard
1 teaspoon rice vinegar
1 teaspoon soy sauce
1 teaspoon ginger, grated

Preparation:

Cook the eggs in the air fryer at 260 degrees for 15 minutes.
Peel and scoop out the yolks.
Add the yolks and the rest of the ingredients in a food processor.
Pulse until smooth.
Add the yolk mixture on top of the egg whites.

Serving Suggestion:

Garnish with sesame seeds.

Tip:

You can also mash the eggs using a fork and stir in the rest of the ingredients if you don't have a food processor.

Nutritional Information Per Serving:

Calories: 63
Total Fat: 5.3g
Saturated Fat: 1.0g
Cholesterol: 94mg

Sodium: 102mg
Potassium: 42mg
Total Carbohydrates: 0.8g

Dietary Fiber: 0.1g
Protein: 3.3g
Sugars: 0g

Spring Rolls

Serves: 16
Preparation and Cooking Time: 35 minutes

Ingredients:

- 1 teaspoon oil
- 1/4 cup onion, diced
- 2 cloves garlic, minced
- 1/2 cup green onion, chopped
- 1/2 cup carrots, shredded
- 1 lb. sausage, crumbled
- 1/2 cup chestnuts, chopped
- Salt and pepper to taste
- 16 spring roll wrappers
- Cooking spray

1. **Preparation:**

2. Add oil to a pan over medium heat.
3. Stir in the rest of the ingredients except the wrappers.
4. Cook for 10 minutes, stirring frequently.
5. Drain the oil.
6. Put the mixture on top of the wrappers.
7. Roll the wrapper and seal.
8. Spray each roll with oil.
9. Cook in the air fryer at 390 degrees F for 4 minutes.
10. Flip and cook for another 4 minutes.

Serving Suggestion:

Serve with soy sauce and vinegar dip.

Tip:

You can also use ground pork instead of sausage.

Nutritional Information Per Serving:

Calories: 98
Total Fat: 5.5g
Saturated Fat: 2.0g
Cholesterol: 12mg
Sodium: 471mg
Potassium: 103mg
Total Carbohydrates: 7.2g
Dietary Fiber: 0.5g
Protein: 4.8g
Sugars: 1g

Eggplant Mini Pizza

Serves: 8
Preparation and Cooking Time: 45 minutes

Ingredients:

- 1 eggplant, sliced into rounds
- Salt to taste
- 1 egg, beaten
- 1 tablespoon water
- 1/4 cup Parmesan cheese, grated
- 1 cup breadcrumbs
- Cooking spray
- 4 oz. pizza sauce
- 8 oz. mozzarella cheese

Preparation:

1. Season both sides of eggplant with salt.
2. Marinate for 10 minutes.
3. In a bowl, mix the egg and water.
4. In another, mix the Parmesan cheese and breadcrumbs.
5. Dip the eggplant in the eggs and then in the breadcrumb mixture.
6. Spray with oil.
7. Cook in the air fryer at 350 degrees F until golden.
8. Take them out of the air fryer.
9. Spread top with the pizza sauce.
10. Top with the cheese.
11. Cook in the air fryer until the cheese has melted.

Serving Suggestion:

Garnish with chopped basil.

Nutritional Information Per Serving:

Calories: 178
Total Fat: 7.6g
Saturated Fat: 4.0g
Cholesterol: 44mg
Sodium: 486mg
Potassium: 221mg
Total Carbohydrates: 16.4g
Dietary Fiber: 3.4g
Protein: 11.4g
Sugars: 3g

Tater Tots

Serves: 4
Preparation and Cooking Time: 15 minutes

Ingredients:

- 36 frozen potato nuggets

Preparation:

1. Preheat your air fryer to 350 degrees F.
2. Add the potato nuggets in the air fryer.
3. Cook for 6 minutes.
4. Shake and cook for another 4 minutes.

Serving Suggestion:

Serve with ketchup.

Nutritional Information Per Serving:

Calories: 110
Total Fat: 6.1g
Saturated Fat: 1.0g
Cholesterol: 0mg
Sodium: 258mg
Potassium: 167mg
Total Carbohydrates: 15.9g
Dietary Fiber: 1.5g
Protein: 1.5g
Sugars: 0g

Chapter 9: 15 Desserts and Snacks

Mini Apple Pies

Serves: 4
Preparation and Cooking Time: 45 minutes

Ingredients:

- 2 apples, diced
- 6 tablespoons brown sugar
- 1 teaspoon ground cinnamon
- 4 tablespoons butter
- 2 teaspoons cold water
- 1 teaspoon cornstarch
- 14 oz. pastry crust pie
- Cooking spray
- 1/2 tablespoon oil

Preparation:

1. Mix the apples, sugar, cinnamon and butter in a pan over medium heat.
2. Cook for 5 minutes, stirring frequently.
3. In a bowl, mix water and cornstarch.
4. Add this to the pan and cook for 1 minute.
5. Transfer apple mixture to a bowl. Let cool.
6. Spread out the pie crust on your kitchen table.
7. Slice into small rectangles.
8. Add filling in the center of each rectangle.
9. Place another rectangle on top.
10. Press the edges with a fork and seal.
11. Spray the air fryer basket with oil.
12. Brush both sides of the apple pie with oil.
13. Bake in the air fryer at 385 degrees F for 8 minutes.

Tip:

You can serve these either warm or room temperature.

Nutritional Information Per Serving:

Calories: 498
Total Fat: 28.6g
Saturated Fat: 11.0g
Cholesterol: 31mg
Sodium: 328mg
Potassium: 152mg
Total Carbohydrates: 59.8g
Dietary Fiber: 3.5g
Protein: 3.3g
Sugars: 36g

Donut Sticks

Serves: 8
Preparation and Cooking Time: 35 minutes

Ingredients:

- 8 oz. crescent roll dough
- 1/4 cup butter
- 2 teaspoons ground cinnamon
- 1/2 cup sugar

Preparation:

1. Spread out the crescent roll dough sheet into a pan.
2. Cut into sticks.
3. Dip each of the sticks in butter.
4. Add to the air fryer basket
5. Cook at 380 degrees F for 5 minutes.
6. Mix the cinnamon and sugar in a bowl.
7. Dust the donut sticks with this mixture.

Serving Suggestion:

Serve with honey or syrup.

Tip:

Store in airtight jar for up to 3 days.

Nutritional Information Per Serving:

Calories: 266
Total Fat: 11.8g
Saturated Fat: 5.0g
Cholesterol: 15mg
Sodium: 267mg
Potassium: 20mg
Total Carbohydrates: 37.6g
Dietary Fiber: 0.5g
Protein: 2.2g
Sugars: 24g

Mini Choco Chip Cookies

Serves: 16
Preparation and Cooking Time: 40 minutes

Ingredients:

- 1/2 cup butter
- 1/2 cup brown sugar
- 1/4 cup white sugar
- 1/2 teaspoon salt
- 1/2 teaspoon baking soda
- 1-1/2 teaspoons vanilla extract
- 1 egg
- 1-1/4 cups all-purpose flour
- 1 cup chocolate chips
- 1/4 cup almonds, chopped

Preparation:

1. Beat the butter in a bowl using electric mixer for 30 seconds on high speed.
2. Stir in the sugars, salt and baking soda.
3. Beat on medium speed for 3 minutes.
4. Add the vanilla and egg.
5. Stir in the flour and continue mixing.
6. Stir in the chocolate chips and almonds.
7. Form cookies into the air fryer basket.
8. Cook at 300 degrees F for 8 minutes.

Serving Suggestion:

Let cool before serving.

Tip:

There's no need to preheat the air fryer.

Nutritional Information Per Serving:

Calories: 188
Total Fat: 10.4g
Saturated Fat: 5.0g
Cholesterol: 24mg
Sodium: 151mg

Potassium: 71mg
Total Carbohydrates: 23.6g
Dietary Fiber: 1.1g
Protein: 2g
Sugars: 15g

Roasted Bananas

Serves: 1
Preparation and Cooking Time: 10 minutes

Ingredients:

- 1 banana, sliced
- Cooking spray

Preparation:

1. Cover your air fryer basket with parchment paper.
2. Preheat your air fryer to 375 degrees F.
3. Add the bananas to the basket.
4. Spray with oil.
5. Cook for 5 minutes.
6. Shake the basket a little.
7. Cook for another 3 minutes.

Serving Suggestion:

Serve with ice cream.

Nutritional Information Per Serving:

Calories: 107
Total Fat: 0.7g
Saturated Fat: 0.0g
Cholesterol: 0mg
Sodium: 1mg
Potassium: 422mg
Total Carbohydrates: 27g
Dietary Fiber: 3.1g
Protein: 1.3g
Sugars: 14g

Apple Fritters

Serves: 4
Preparation and Cooking Time: 25 minutes

Ingredients:

- Cooking spray
- 1 cup all-purpose flour
- 1-1/2 teaspoons baking powder
- 1 egg
- Salt to taste
  1/4 cup white sugar
- 1/4 cup milk
- 1/2 teaspoon ground cinnamon
- 2 tablespoons white sugar
- 1 apple, chopped

Preparation:

1. Preheat your air fryer to 350 degrees F.
2. Spray the air fryer basket with oil.
3. In a bowl, combine the flour, baking powder, egg, salt, ¼ cup white sugar and milk.
4. Mix well.

5. In another bowl, blend the cinnamon and remaining sugar.
6. Toss the apples in this mixture.
7. Add the apples to the flour mixture.
8. Use a cookie scoop and drop mixture into the air fryer basket.
9. Cook for 5 minutes.
10. Flip and cook for another 5 minutes.

Serving Suggestion:

Drizzle with honey before serving.

Nutritional Information Per Serving:

Calories: 297
Total Fat: 2.1g
Saturated Fat: 1.0g
Cholesterol: 48mg
Sodium: 248mg
Potassium: 119mg
Total Carbohydrates: 64.9g
Dietary Fiber: 1.9g
Protein: 5.5g
Sugars: 39g

Butter Cake

Serves: 4
Preparation and Cooking Time: 30 minutes

Ingredients:

- Cooking spray
- 7 tablespoons butter
- 1/4 cup sugar
- 1 egg
- 1-1/4 cups all-purpose flour
- Pinch salt
- 6 tablespoons milk

Preparation:

1. Preheat your air fryer to 350 degrees F.
2. Spray cake pan with oil.
3. Beat butter and sugar using an electric mixer until mixture becomes creamy.
4. Stir in eggs.
5. Mix until smooth.
6. Add the flour and salt.
7. Mix well.
8. Transfer mixture into the pan.
9. Add the pan to the air fryer.
10. Cook for 15 minutes.

Tip:

Stick a toothpick into the cake. If it comes clean, it means that the cake is done.

Nutritional Information Per Serving:

Calories: 470
Total Fat: 22.4g
Saturated Fat: 14.0g
Cholesterol: 102mg
Sodium: 210mg
Potassium: 113mg
Total Carbohydrates: 59.7g
Dietary Fiber: 1.4g
Protein: 7.9g
Sugars: 20g

Banana Chips

Serves: 2

Preparation and Cooking Time: 20 minutes

Ingredients:

- 1 banana, sliced into chips
- Cooking spray

Preparation:

1. Preheat your air fryer to 350 degrees F.
2. Spray air fryer basket with oil.
3. Add the banana slices to the basket.
4. Spray the banana with oil.
5. Cook for 8 to 9 minutes.
6. Flip and cook for another 3 minutes.

Serving Suggestion:

Toss in cinnamon sugar before serving.

Nutritional Information Per Serving:

Calories: 109
Total Fat: 0.3g
Saturated Fat: 0.0g
Cholesterol: 0mg
Sodium: 81mg
Potassium: 447mg
Total Carbohydrates: 28.5g
Dietary Fiber: 2.1g
Protein: 1.2g
Sugars: 13g

Banana Cake

Serves: 4
Preparation and Cooking Time: 40 minutes

Ingredients:

- Cooking spray
- 3 tablespoons butter
- 1/4 cup brown sugar
- 1 egg
- 1 banana, mashed
- 2 tablespoons honey
- 1/2 teaspoon ground cinnamon
- Pinch salt
- 1 cup self-rising flour

Preparation:

1. Preheat your air fryer to 320 degrees F.
2. Spray a small cake pan with oil.
3. Beat the butter and sugar in a bowl using electric mixer.
4. In another bowl, mix the egg, banana and honey.
5. Add egg mixture to butter mixture.
6. Mix well.
7. Stir in cinnamon, salt and flour.
8. Pour mixture into a cake pan.
9. Add cake pan to the air fryer basket.
10. Cook for 30 minutes.

Tip:

Insert toothpick into the cake to see if it's done.

Nutritional Information Per Serving:

Calories: 347
Total Fat: 11.8g
Saturated Fat: 7.0g
Cholesterol: 73mg
Sodium: 531mg
Potassium: 195mg
Total Carbohydrates: 56.9g
Dietary Fiber: 1.8g
Protein: 5.2g
Sugars: 30g

Beignets

Serves: 7

Preparation and Cooking Time: 25 minutes

Ingredients:

- Cooking spray
- 1/4 cup white sugar
- 1/2 cup all-purpose flour
- 1 egg, yolk separated from white
- 1/8 cup water
- 1/2 teaspoon baking powder
- 1-1/2 teaspoons butter, melted
- 1/2 teaspoon vanilla extract
- Pinch salt

Preparation:

1. Preheat your air fryer to 370 degrees F.
2. Spray muffin molds with oil.
3. In a bowl, mix all the ingredients except the egg white.
4. Transfer egg white to a bowl and beat with electric mixer on medium speed until you see soft peaks forming.
5. Gradually add this to the batter.
6. Pour the batter into the molds.
7. Add the molds to the air fryer basket.
8. Cook for 10 minutes.
9. Remove from the molds and flip into the air fryer basket.
10. Cook for 4 more minutes.

Serving Suggestion:

Dust with confectioners' sugar.

Nutritional Information Per Serving:

Calories: 88
Total Fat: 1.7g
Saturated Fat: 1.0g
Cholesterol: 29mg
Sodium: 74mg
Potassium: 20mg
Total Carbohydrates: 16.2g
Dietary Fiber: 0.2g
Protein: 1.8g
Sugars: 9g

Fried Oreos

Serves: 9

Preparation and Cooking Time: 10 minutes

Ingredients:

- 1/2 cup pancake mix
- 1/3 cup water
- Cooking spray
- 9 Oreos

Preparation:

1. Combine pancake mix and water.
2. Cover air fryer basket with parchment paper.
3. Spray with oil.
4. Dip the oreos in the pancake mixture.
5. Add to the basket.
6. Preheat your air fryer to 400 degrees F.
7. Cook for 5 minutes.
8. Flip and cook for another 3 minutes.

Serving Suggestion:

Dust with confectioners' sugar.

Tip:

Make sure Oreos do not overlap inside the air fryer.

Nutritional Information Per Serving:

Calories: 77
Total Fat: 2.1g
Saturated Fat: 0.0g
Cholesterol: 0mg

Sodium: 156mg
Potassium: 31mg
Total Carbohydrates: 13.7g
Dietary Fiber: 0.3g
Protein: 1.2g
Sugars: 5g

Cinnamon Donuts

Serves: 9
Preparation and Cooking Time: 40 minutes

Ingredients:

2-1/2 tablespoons butter
1/2 cup white sugar
2 egg yolks
1 teaspoon salt
1-1/2 teaspoons baking powder
2-1/4 cups all-purpose flour
1/2 cup sour cream, divided
1 teaspoon cinnamon
1/4 cup white sugar
2 tablespoons melted butter

Preparation:

Combine butter and white sugar until you form crumbly mixture.
Stir in the egg yolk and mix well.
In another bowl, mix the salt, baking powder and flour.
Add the flour mixture and sour cream to the egg mixture.
Mix well.
Refrigerate the dough for 15 minutes.
While waiting, mix the cinnamon and remaining sugar in a bowl.
Spread out the dough on your kitchen table.
Cut circles using a cookie cutter.
Cut another smaller circle in the center to form a donut.
Preheat your air fryer to 350 degrees F.
Brush both sides of donuts with melted butter.
Cook donuts for 8 minutes.

Serving Suggestion:

Serve warm.

Nutritional Information Per Serving:

Calories: 276
Total Fat: 9.7g
Saturated Fat: 6.0g
Cholesterol: 66mg
Sodium: 390mg
Potassium: 59mg
Total Carbohydrates: 43.5g
Dietary Fiber: 1g
Protein: 4.3g
Sugars: 19g

Cherry Crumble

Serves: 4

Preparation and Cooking Time: 1 hour and 10 minutes

Ingredients:

- 1/4 cup butter
- 3 cups cherries, pitted
- 2 teaspoons freshly squeezed lemon juice
- 10 tablespoons white sugar, divided
- 1 cup all-purpose flour
- 1 teaspoon ground cinnamon
- 1 teaspoon ground nutmeg
- 1 teaspoon vanilla powder

Preparation:

1. Slice the butter into smaller cubes.
2. Freeze butter cubes for 15 minutes.
3. Preheat your air fryer to 325 degrees F.
4. Mix the cherries, lemon juice and 2 tablespoons sugar.
5. Blend well.
6. Pour this mixture into a baking pan.
7. Combine flour and 6 tablespoons sugar.
8. Add butter to the flour and spread mixture on top of the cherries.
9. Mix the remaining sugar, cinnamon, nutmeg and vanilla.
10. Sprinkle this mixture on top of the cherries.
11. Bake in the air fryer for 25 minutes.

Serving Suggestion:

Let cool for 10 minutes before serving.

Nutritional Information Per Serving:

Calories: 459
Total Fat: 17.8g
Saturated Fat: 10.0g
Cholesterol: 41mg
Sodium: 109mg
Potassium: 257mg
Total Carbohydrates: 76.4g
Dietary Fiber: 6.4g
Protein: 4.9g
Sugars: 49g

Corn Nuts

Serves: 8

Preparation and Cooking Time: 9 hours and 15 minutes

Ingredients:

- 14 oz. white corn
- 3 tablespoons oil
- 1-1/2 teaspoons salt

Preparation:

1. Soak corn in water for 8 hours.
2. Drain and spread on a baking pan.
3. Let dry for 20 minutes.
4. Preheat your air fryer to 400 degrees F.
5. Toss the corn in oil and sprinkle with salt.
6. Cook in the air fryer for 10 minutes.
7. Shake and cook for another 10 minutes.
8. Shake again and cook for 5 minutes.

Serving Suggestion:

Sprinkle with ranch powder or Cajun seasoning before serving.

Tip:

Store in an airtight jar for up to 3 days.

Nutritional Information Per Serving:

Calories: 225
Total Fat: 7.4g
Saturated Fat: 1.0g
Cholesterol: 0mg
Sodium: 438mg

Potassium: 141mg
Total Carbohydrates: 35.8g
Dietary Fiber: 7g
Protein: 5.9g
Sugars: 1g

Salty & Sour Chickpeas

Serves: 2
Preparation and Cooking Time: 50 minutes

Ingredients:

- 1 cup white vinegar
- 15 oz. canned chickpeas, rinsed and drained
- 1 tablespoon olive oil
- Salt to taste

Preparation:

1. Pour vinegar into a pan over medium low heat.
2. Stir in chickpeas and simmer for 30 minutes.
3. Drain chickpeas.
4. Preheat your air fryer to 390 degrees F.
5. Add chickpeas to the air fryer basket.
6. Cook for 4 minutes.
7. Add chickpeas to a bowl and toss in oil and salt.
8. Put the chickpeas back to the air fryer.
9. Cook for another 8 minutes, shaking every 2 minutes.

Serving Suggestion:

Serve immediately.

Tip:

When the chickpeas lose crunchy texture, reheat in the air fryer for 1 minute.

Nutritional Information Per Serving:

Calories: 229
Total Fat: 8.3g
Saturated Fat: 1.0g
Cholesterol: 0mg
Sodium: 859mg
Potassium: 244mg
Total Carbohydrates: 31.7g
Dietary Fiber: 6.2g
Protein: 6.9g
Sugars: 0g

Pumpkin Seeds

Serves: 6
Preparation and Cooking Time: 1 hour

Ingredients:

- 1-3/4 cups pumpkin seeds
- 2 teaspoons olive oil
- 1 teaspoon salt
- 1 teaspoon paprika

Preparation:

1. Add pumpkin seeds to a strainer.
2. Rinse and drain.

3. Dry the seeds using paper towels.
4. Preheat your air fryer to 350 degrees F.
5. Toss the seeds in oil, salt and paprika.
6. Add to the air fryer basket.
7. Cook for 35 minutes, shaking every 10 minutes.

Tip:

Check the pumpkin seeds 25 to 30 minutes after you started cooking to avoid burning.

Nutritional Information Per Serving:

Calories: 233
Total Fat: 20.2g
Saturated Fat: 4.0g
Cholesterol: 0mg
Sodium: 395mg
Potassium: 333mg
Total Carbohydrates: 7.4g
Dietary Fiber: 1.6g
Protein: 9.9g
Sugars: 0g

Conclusion

Pull-off Crispy and Healthy Meals From Thin Air

One of the main selling points of air fryers is its promise of cooking healthier and tasty food by using little to no oil. Doing so has never been this easy with Ninja Air Fryer Max XL.

The Ninja Air Fryer Max serves up many uses in meal preparation making it as convenient and healthy as possible for any household. Talking about convenience, the air fryer does all the cooking and all you have to do is to wait for the beep. It does not only work as a fryer but also offers other cooking functions that make cooking a lot easier. It broils, bakes, dehydrates, reheats food and more easily without the fuss with its easy to use functions that anyone in the household can operate. It's an all in one combination.

Its sleek design makes any kitchen look professional and its functions making it a reliable help in the kitchen. Equipped with sturdy materials, this air fryer has many great things to offer. Like a real ninja, this air fryer does more than any other air fryers out there.

Air fryers basically work via the same principle of convection, so one issue when it comes to air fryers is their capacity. It needs to have adequate space inside the unit for hot air to circulate and flow evenly around the food. Therefore, you will have to work on small batches and won't be filling the basket to get nice and even browned food. When it comes to capacity, Ninja Air Fryer Max XL offers enough capacity to hold a good batch of ingredients of up to 3 pounds of French fries so your family can enjoy the food right away.

Many people enjoy the idea of consuming a healthier version of what used to be health-risky and fattening foods. With Ninja Air Fryer Max XL you can enjoy the fact that no oil is needed to cook your food. With the promise of little to no oil added in frying foods while making it remain delicious without the guilt, the air fryer is a perfect appliance for those looking to switch to a healthier lifestyle.

CPSIA information can be obtained
at www.ICGtesting.com
Printed in the USA
LVHW062227090421
684057LV00002B/157

9 781954 294844